Big Carp Legends

Bountyhunter
Publications

First published in 2012
By Bountyhunter Publications
© Bountyhunter Publications 2012

ISBN 978-0-9569800-0-7
Printed in Great Britain

Big Carp Legends

Rob Maylin

Bountyhunter
Publications

Contents

𝔇𝔢𝔡𝔦𝔠𝔞𝔱𝔦𝔬𝔫

This book is dedicated to my long time angling buddy Rob McGill who died in 2011 aged only 59.

Rob and I fished together for over 20 years at Yateley, Swan, Frimley, Horseshoe and Sandhurst. He was one of life's good guys, who could bring a smile to your face even when things were getting you down. Loved by everyone who knew him, but none more than me. I'm going to miss him so much on the bank and in the pub. It's hard to imagine life without him.

RIP Rob and save me a swim at that magical lake in the sky. No doubt I'll be seeing you one day soon.

Foreword by Rob Maylin

Born in Bedfordshire in 1956, my interest in fishing came from my father, Jeff. A keen angler, his grandfather once owned 'Maylin's Pool' or Withy Pool as it's known today, situated in the small village of Henlow. At three years old, my father was already taking me night fishing to Henlow, although in those days we drove the car to the water's edge and float-fished for tench by the light of the headlamps! My father also worked at Vauxhall, and we both joined the angling club, enabling us to fish at Woburn, Linford Lakes and the River Ouse around Radwell. It wasn't long before I was in their match team and fishing up and down the country.

I took a fancy to barbel in the late sixties and spent some time fishing The Royalty at Christchurch, and later on The Severn around Bridgnorth where a fishing holiday led to me getting together with the landlady's daughter. Over a couple of years while I was in my late teens, I caught hundreds of barbel, and I suppose I got them out of my system.

Carp were next on the agenda, and with little written about them and even less tackle available, I was back to Henlow fishing Maylin's and another pool up the road called the Airman. Vauxhall had several carp lakes: Woburn Sands and Wyboston in the early days, then around 1970 they purchased Stanton Hardcourt in Oxfordshire. I fished all of these before I caught my first twenty. I think I had four twenties from Arlesey Lake that year in 1972. I fished Arlesey on and off for several years and also moved slightly further afield to Stanborough and Fairlands in Hertfordshire around the birth of the boilie in the mid-seventies.

By 1980 I had fished Savay on a day ticket and in 1983 joined the 'Loony Rota' where suddenly my fishing life changed in favour of beer and nightlife. Waveney Valley saw my first capture of a thirty in 1983, and the second a week or so later from Duncan Kay's Mid-Northants Carp Fishery. Now I was on a roll and in search of waters that held a 35lb-plus. It was then that a ticket for North Harrow Waltonians came up. I was very successful here and caught a lot of thirties, enough I thought to write my first book, Tiger Bay. I fished Savay for several years until we, the 'Famous Five', were banned. So it was off to pastures new – Yateley's Copse Lake and North Lake, Longfield and Farlows.

Always on the lookout for the next big fish, The Snake Pit, Broadlands, Johnson's, Harefield and Pit 3 all succumbed to our ruthless approach. Until in 1991, after making Harefield Haulin' with Stuart Gillham, I was Yateley-bound in search of a forty, with a little stop-off at Stanstead Abbotts to put

8

my name on the 'Big One' in there. Fox Pool was written, along with Carp for Beekay Publishers.

Bazil took some catching, but after a two-year campaign, she was mine, and the Pad Lake seemed the obvious choice (while finishing off my fourth book, Bazil's Bush, and launching Big Carp magazine by the way). With the Pad Lake done and dusted, I moved the bivvy 10ft into the Island swim on the Car Park and spent two very enjoyable years fishing virtually full-time.

A run-in with the Environment Agency at Colnemere did my head in and blew me away so much so that I didn't fish for three years, but instead went on a clubbing marathon, doing London three nights a week at Camden Palace etc and any Frantic nights, every festival and half a dozen trips to Ibiza. It's true to say that I did it properly, and dropped from 18 to 12 stone by the way! With that 'out of the way' I went back to fishing when Swan did its first 40lb common. That first year back, I had the 40lb common twice and 20 thirties by only doing day sessions. So a decision to pack away the bivvy and buy some maggots was made. Frimley was next, all done and dusted in a week, and then Menards, Horseshoe and Sandhurst all received

First 30, Waveney Valley 1983.

Harrow off the Lawn.

One of the Fox Pool's A-Team.

Yateley gold.

the mag-aligner treatment over the next few years.

Today, well, I'm back to 18 stone, and fishing for enjoyment only, not because I have to, and enjoying life along the way as usual. There's a saying, 'been there, done that and bought the T-shirt' – well as you can see, I certainly have. In fact I've bought the T-shirt in XXL down to medium, then back to XXL again. Here's hoping I don't have to get XXXL, but you never know – fishing's a funny old game!

Most of what I've put in a nutshell here, I've written about before. The Yateley days were of course relived in my latest book, 2009's 'One Last Cast', but what I never wrote about was a lot of the controversial stuff that went on. My ban from the North Harrow Waltonians, what really happened at Savay with me and the 'Famous Five', our wild nights out around the country, and the truth behind all the rumours and lies. Now here's your chance to know what really happened. Were we as bad as everyone made out? Bloody right we were, and then some! Read on... (But please don't judge me too hard; I'm an old man now and very sorry, honest!).

Introduction
The Early Years

"I was very lucky as a small child to have a father who was a keen angler and a great grandfather who had his own carp lake."

I was very lucky as a small child to have a father who was a keen angler, and for that matter, a great grandfather who had his own carp lake. Back in the early 60's, carp fishing was very much in its infancy even though Richard Walker and his pals had been doing it for a few years, there were very few carp anglers out there and it was all very hush-hush and top secret.

My father worked for Vauxhall Motors in Luton. At that time the car plant had about 30,000 people working there and Luton was a very affluent part of the country. They had a huge fishing club with thousands of members and rented waters, both rivers and stillwaters, up and down the country. In later years they were even able to purchase their own lakes such as the Stanton Harcourt Carp Fishery in Oxford, which was purchased in the early 70's.

My father was very keen on tench and carp, but tench I suppose were his real favourites, and the venues that he took me to at a very early age, probably only three or four years old, were the Pool Café at Henlow, which was owned by his grandfather at the time, and was a deep clay pit that had a submerged forest in it. On the opposite side of the road to the Henlow Royal Airforce base, the airmen used to use the lake for swimming in the 50's and 60's, and the lake had a couple of diving boards on it. Unfortunately in the 60's a young airman was drowned having got caught up in all these old trees that littered the bottom of the lake, and swimming was prohibited from then on.

There were a stock of carp in the lake, probably about 20 old warriors, and quite a few of the well known carp anglers of the day fished at the Pool Café, including both Richard Walker and Jack Hilton. The lake was known as Maylin's Pool at the time, and they wished to keep the venue a secret, so they came up with the name Junelin's because the season began on the 16th June. Throughout their early writings, both in the old Drop Me A Line series in the Angling Times and in their early books, you will see references to Junelin's. This in fact was my great grandfather's lake, the Pool Café, which was purchased by Kevin Maddocks in the mid 80's and its name changed to Withy Pool. There's still a syndicate on the lake now, which is run by Brenda Maddocks I believe.

The café sat just off the road with a large car park behind it and then the lake, so my father would drive his car right to the edge of the lake and shine his car headlights onto the surface of the water, enabling him and his friends to float fish even during the middle of the night. Bearing in mind this was late 50's and early 60's, at the time it wasn't frowned upon, but I would like to see what people would think of this down on the Car Park Lake down at Yateley these days. If you were to drive your car up to the water's edge and put your headlights across the lake, I'm sure there would be a few letters of complaints in to HQ, but at the time it was the done thing and my father caught some huge tench from the lake. I never saw him catch a carp, but I did see carp swimming in the lake, and even at that young age they had a certain mystery about them.

The other venue that my father loved for tench fishing was Woburn Sands – two large chalk pits or clay pits I believe, which were rented by Vauxhall Angling Club. Both of these lakes were again very deep with water in excess of 20ft. The top lake, which I believe was filled in in the late 80's, was known as the Shovel, as the shape of the lake resembles a spade or shovel. The large lake held the majority of the carp but was known to be very difficult. I did see my father catch some carp from the Shovel way back in probably the late 60's on floatfished bread. At the time there were a number of BCSG members fishing these lakes for the carp. One chap's name I remember was Eddy Peacock, and he was a well-known carp angler in the Bedford area. The other whose surname escapes me, had the nickname of Big Frank, and it was Big Frank who I first spoke to over at Woburn Sands way back in the 60's. I remember that all his tackle was painted matt black; the rods were matt black, the reels, the bank sticks – everything. He had one of the old Send Marketing brolly camps up as did a few of his friends who were all freelining large lumps of paste. I was intrigued to watch them fish, and couldn't quite understand what they were doing at the time. They would tie a large weight on the end of the line and cast right across the lake onto the opposite bank and then walk round, tie on a hook and squeeze on a large knob of cat food paste, gently dropping it into the far margins. With freelining tactics, obviously this left a lot to be desired as far as indication was concerned. They would quickly run round and try and tighten the line up without moving the large knob of paste from the far margins, but if there was any sort of surface wind at all on the lake, this was very difficult.

The indicators as I remember were modified Heron bite alarms with pieces of silver paper as bobbins. I actually watched Frank fishing that first day I saw him, tearing his silver paper in half telling me that it was too heavy for the eels that he was fishing for. He had several large rusk sacks submerged in the margins in front of his swim, which he reliably told me were full of eels. He and his friends were very partial to jellied eels, and they would take the eels from the lake. Little did I know in my naivety that it was actually carp in the sacks and they were moving the carp from the Shovel Lake through a copse of trees by the side of the Shovel onto another lake, which was within the grounds of a plastic bottle factory known as Plysu. This lake obviously had a large head of carp, which had been moved from surrounding venues. Although the movement of carp these days is massively frowned upon, in those days, and we're talking the 60's and 70's, it seemed fairly acceptable, and as long as the fish measured up to the size indicated on your rod licence, you were able to take them away with you, dead or alive.

Of course these guys had the fishing rights to the lake within the factory grounds and they were stocking it up. This is the way all the lakes were stocked in the early days, especially around the Bedfordshire area, which became a bit of a hotbed for early days carp fishing. Of course, Richard Walker lived in both Flitwick and Biggleswade, so carp fishing was well known in that area, and a lot of the top carp anglers of that day lived around there and wrote letters backwards and forwards to Richard about their carp fishing exploits.

By 1964 at the age of eight, a carp is what I wanted to catch more than anything else in the world. This was brought about by a fishing trip organised by my father and another BCSG member whose name once again I don't know, but his nickname I remember was Scrub Nut as he had a very short haircut. At the time he was a keen carp angler, one of the top guys at the time, and he took my father and I over to a lake at Sharpenhoe in Bedfordshire called the PTA Tool Factory Lake, another lake in the factory grounds. I think a lot of these factories had lakes within their grounds, which were probably dug for the workers to fish as a hobby, but of course the workforce would all go out in the summer and sit round the lake with their sandwiches, throw lumps of bread in and watch these carp coming up feeding from them. Anyway on this particular session we fished during the day for the small tench, which abounded in the lake. I've never fished a lake in my life with so many tiny little tench in there, anything from an ounce to a pound, and you could catch them all day long float fishing with flour and water paste. In the evening my father came and got me and said we were going to sit behind Scrub and he was going to fish for carp with floating crust. It was the catalyst that started a fire within me that's still burning now, some 40 years later. Well into darkness, and after seeing several swirls at Scrub's crust, suddenly he tightened up, his centrepin reel burst into life, and after a fight that seemed to go on forever, probably half an hour or more, he landed a superb common carp of 18lb. I was only a boy at the time and remember as we pulled up outside our house my mother coming to the front door and me running up the drive with my mouth wide open. I just couldn't wait to tell her about the spectacle that I had beheld and the first thing I blurted out of my mouth was "Moby Dick, Moby Dick... Scrub caught Moby Dick," and a picture of that fish is still etched upon my mind now. I

(Above) Early setup.
(Left) My diary from 1972, full of carp secrets!

My Vauxhall Angling Club cards from the early seventies, to fish Woburn Sands, Wyboston and Stanton Hardcourt.

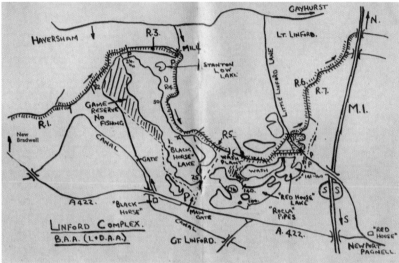

The Linford Complex as it was in 1974.

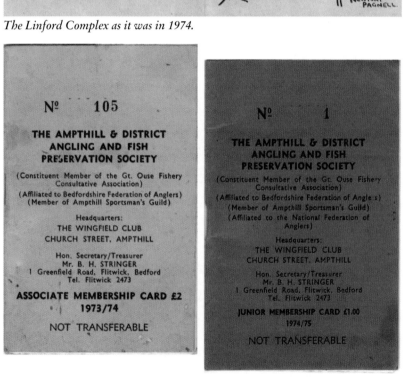

Amphil & District permits 1973 and 1974 to fish Kempston Hardwick.

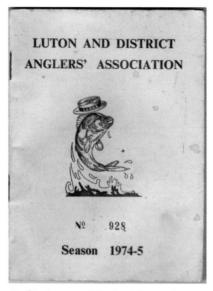

(Left) Luton & District AA permit, 1974-75 to fish Linford Lakes.
(Right) Kempston Angling Club permit 1974.

Arlesey Lake – 'The Logs'.

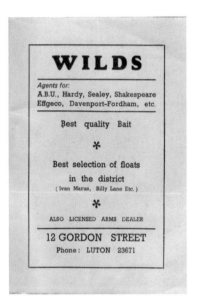

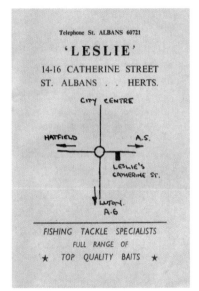

(Left)   Wilds, where I worked as a boy in Luton.
(Right)   Early advert for 'Leslie', yet to move to Luton, where I also worked as a
Saturday boy alongside Matt Hayes and Max Cottis.

22lb, Arlesey.

can see it as if it was yesterday, such was the impact that huge fish made upon me.

At the age of 12, I had begun working in my local fishing tackle shop on Saturdays and after school. A lovely guy who ran the fishing section, Harry Eddington happened to be a friend of my father's, and one Saturday my dad took me in and asked him if he would mind looking after me for the day on Saturdays and letting me work behind the counter. I was like a kid in a sweet shop; it was amazing to listen to the stories of the older guys, many of whom were fishing for carp at the time, and others who were keen on the match fishing in the area. Vauxhall Angling Club had a big match section and they ran a coach every Sunday, which picked up in about a dozen places around the Luton area, for anyone who wanted to go along to the match. As my father didn't want to fish every weekend, this is the route that I took, and I would walk down the hill, down Farley Hill, from where I lived in Luton with all my tackle every Sunday morning at around 4am. I remember the weight of it on my shoulders and almost retching by the time I got to the bus stop.

There'd be a couple of other guys there too sometimes at my stop waiting for the coach to come along, the Vauxhall coach, and one of them was Richard Smith who became a well known fishing and wildlife artist. We remained friends and still are friends to this day, and he actually painted the pictures that became the covers of my first two books, Tiger Bay and Fox Pool. I remember sitting there on the corner of Meyrick Avenue and London Road waiting for the coach to appear, with big smiles on our faces listening to the stories of some of the older guys who were in the coach, and who had been out the night before, on the beer and on the pull. They would have very colourful stories to say the least about some of the ladies they had met in the local clubs and the things they had got up to, with some of them barely making the coach that morning having spent the night around a girl's house. To hear these stories at the age of ten and 12 years old certainly opened my eyes to the world, and was a fantastic start for my fishing.

There were two or three other teenagers who worked in Wilds the tackle shop that were keen carp fishermen They too were fishing over at Henlow, but in the lake just up the road from Withy Pool, or Maylin's Pool as it was known at the time – a lake known as the Airman Pool. As I told you earlier there was an airfield across the other side of the road, which had airmen from the UK and from the US. For some reason there were a lot of US airmen in this area, and Chicksands airbase was not far away. I remember listening to their stories of parboiled potatoes and cat food specials up on this Airman Pool, which was another deep lake by the way.

One day there were big celebrations within the shop, and we were all taken across the road to the Bute Street Milk Bar. It's funny, you don't see these places these days, but there were actually cafés that specialised in milk and milkshake drinks, and a lot of the teenagers would end up in there. The reason for the celebrations was that one of the guys had caught a 20lb carp – 21lb 10oz. I still remember the weight even though I was probably no more than ten or 12 years old. I mean this was a big carp for the day; we're talking about the early 70's here, and it was like catching a 50lb'er these days, I suppose.

Anyway, I was very, very fortunate in that working in the tackle shop I got to meet some of the best carp anglers in the area, and a couple of them took me under their wing, one of which was Big Frank. Now Big Frank loved his carp fishing. He wasn't a BCSG member; in fact he was a bit of a rogue if I remember correctly, but he had a car and he was willing to take me fishing. We began our carp fishing down on the Stanton Harcourt venue I spoke about in Oxford in 1970, so I would have been 14 then. We found the carp down the bottom end of the lake on the shallows where the wind was blowing into. We spent the day fishing with floating crust, with the sun in my eyes, and I remember latching into one of these fish, the only one of the day; a fish of around about 5lb, and a lovely scaly little mirror became my first ever carp that was caught by design.

Another passion of Big Frank's was barbel fishing, and he and his pals would go down to the Royalty Fishery at Ringwood and fish on the Hampshire Avon, and I began to get into barbel fishing too. At the time maggots were banned on the Royalty Fishery if you can believe it! Quite why there was a maggot ban I don't know; I suppose people were putting in far too many of the little wrigglers. They certainly wouldn't ban them these days, knowing how nutritious they are for the fish, but at the time maggots were banned. But being a bit of a scallywag, of course that was the bait we wanted to use down there, so when I began to fish the Royalty, we would dig a hole in the bank and put our bait tins in the hole, and then put a large tackle box over the top of the hole and sit there all day long. As soon as the bailiffs had gone by, we put in some large balls of groundbait laced with maggots, and we had some tremendous fishing down there. I'm laughing as I relate this, but I'm really not trying to teach any of the younger readers my bad habits. Then again, you are what you are, and I'm sure you don't want me to hold back on any of the little edges that I had at the time.

So, barbel fishing became a bit of a passion of mine, and I would go down to the Royalty Fishery a couple of times a year for a holiday, staying in the

23lb, Arlesey.

Maylin's Pool, referred to as Junelin's by Dick Walker and later to be called Withy Pool by Kevin Maddocks.

Maylin's Pool – original.

SPECIES: MIRROR CARP.   DATE: 16 TH JUNE 1977. TIME: 4·00 A.M.   WATER: WOBURN SANDS-V.HAC
WEIGHT: 11 lb 10 ozs.
TACKLE: MITCHEL 300; 6oz CARP ROD; 8 lb BAYER PERLON; ½oz ARLSEY BOMB; A.A SHOT
        SIZE 4 ALLCOCKS MODEL PERFECT SHORT SHANK HOOK.
BAIT : 2 NIBLETS OF BEJAM CUT CORN SWEETENED WITH SLIMLIA SUGAR
TACTICS: THE BOMB WAS SUSPENDED 2½FT FROM THE HOOK, AND WAS CAST 8FT
        FROM THE BANK ABOUT 15 YDS FROM THE FROUNT OF THE SHOVEL, ON THE
        LEFT HAND SIDE ADJACENT TO A PATCH OF LILIES ABOUT 5FT X 15 FT, THE
        LINE WAS ALLOWED TO FLOAT ON THE WATER SINCE ODD STEMS CLOSE TO
        THE FROUNT PREVENTED LINE SINK. 3 BAITING UP SESSIONS PRECEEDED
        THIS TRIP.
COMMENTS: TYPICAL RUN, I STRUCK BEFORE REEL HANDLE MOVED. FISH MADE 1 LONG
No. 1   RUN UP THE LEFT BANK, AND GAVE INTENSE CLOSE-IN FIGHT WHICH
         INCLUDED SEVERAL WEEDINGS, AFTER ABOUT 12 MINS THE FISH WAS
         NETTED, PHOTOGRAPHED AND RETURNED. ALSO SAW AN 18 lb FISH TAKEN ON
         FREELINED LOB WORM-10 lb LINE. MIDDLE RIGHT BANK. WATER TEMP. WARMISH.

One of my original "Catch Data Cards' from the seventies.

A quiet corner at Woburn Sands.

Woburn original 1972.

Check out the reel!

Early seventies Woburn double.

bed and breakfasts, normally Mill Stream Cottage if my memory serves me right, and fishing the Avon, wandering up and down, and even on to the Throop as well and having a little go on there.

Once the winter came round, just about everybody changed to pike fishing unless they were in the match scene, and at the time some large gravel pits over at Newport Pagnell were superb pike venues. They were owned originally by Birmingham Angling Club, then Luton Angling Club took them over. In the end, which must have been the late 80's, Len Gurd actually had the fishing rights on there, and they became the Linear Fisheries over at Newport Pagnell, which had a lot of carp in there. We've had many articles in the magazine about them, but in those early days, there weren't any carp in the lakes at all, but pike fishing was very good on there in the winter. Once the beginning of the season was coming round though, it was carp fishing that everybody was talking about.

One of the other guys to take me under his wing was a chap called James Gregg. He was another Luton based BCSG member who had been fishing down at Arlesey Lake, another old stomping ground of Richard Walker's. There are several lakes over in Arlesey, the Blue and Green Lagoons and the Hitchin Angling Club Arlesey Lake by the side of the railway there, and it was the Hitchin Angling Club Lake that had the big carp in.

It contained quite a number of 20lb carp in the early 70's and one 30lb carp too. I was taken over there originally with James, and it must have been around about 1970 or 1971. This guy was one of the top carp anglers at the time; he built his own rods from blanks that he purchased from Alan Brown's tackle shop in Hitchin. Alan Brown's was known throughout the country as a top specialist fishing tackle shop and people would come from all over England to this little shop in Hitchin, which stocked many of the things that we take for granted these days. They were one of the first shops in the country to have the Lafuma low chairs, and even though I was working in Wilds at the time, we certainly didn't stock any of this real specialist stuff of the day; even the blanks for the carp rods could only be purchased over at Alan Brown's. So James kindly took me over there one Saturday morning and I purchased my first carp rod blanks in brown glass on a Hardy blank, if my memory serves me right. They actually had a Hardy carp rod out at the time, one of the first carp rods on the market. Glass was a fairly new material to be used for fishing rods; most of my father's rods were either cane, split cane or tank aerials – yes, the actual metal aerials that were used on the tanks had rings whipped on them and were used as fishing rods. That story I told you about Scrub Nut catching his 18lb common out of the Tool Factory Lake, well that was actually caught on a tank aerial. So

I purchased rings and reel fittings and that carp rod was the first rod that I actually made myself. I went on to make dozens of rods for myself in those early years. People just used to do it, and whipping became something that you learned to do. You could whip the rings on yourself, and glue the reel fittings on with Araldite in the position you wanted them, and the rods were very much exclusive to you.

When it came to bite indicators, the only one that was readily available was the Heron bite alarm. These were a little bit temperamental if it was windy or anything as they just had a little lever that the line was put behind, and as the line tightened, it pulled the lever across and made two contacts touch each other inside, sending out an audible warning and turning on a big red bulb on the front. In the late 70's I actually designed my own bite indicators and had them made at Vauxhall Motors funnily enough. I had some friends and friends of my father's who worked in the design studios there. I actually got a job there in the end after six years at Luton University studying engineering, and I became a draftsman in the design studios. In the prototype build section in the same building, a few friends of mine were busily making lots of fishing tackle, and the little bite indicators that I had made were based on the same contact type alarms as the old Herons, but I just made them a little bit better and they wouldn't go off in the wind. They weren't quite so sensitive, but certainly did the job.

So armed with my new carp rod and my Mitchell 300 reel loaded up with Maxima line, I went off on my first couple of proper carp fishing trips on Arlesey Lake with James Gregg. The methods that were used at the time were crust or balanced crust, which doesn't seem all that exciting these days, but at the time it was pretty high tech. The balanced crust was made by using a piece of crust from a normal loaf of bread and a blob of Pillsbury dough. This is a sort of bread dough for making your own bread that you could squeeze around the shank of the hook and put just enough on so that it sank very slowly into the water, much the same concept as critical balancing that I came up with in the early 80's using pop-ups. There were boilies around I believe, certainly towards the end of the 70's; Fred Wilton had come up with his theory of high nutritional value baits and I'll get on to my first experiences of those in a moment, but at the time no one was using boilies or anything like that. It was all specials as they were known, which were pastes made out of sausage meat or cat food combined with some cereal to hold it together, or bread type baits. Trout pellets became a big favourite as well, though not used in the form we use them today in the pellet form; we would actually scald them with boiling water and put eggs in there and make them into paste. These were the first of the boilies if you like, and they were pretty high nutrition themselves, but this was before the milk proteins or anything like that. Len Gurd and his crew were innovators in that area. Len Gurd also worked at Vauxhall Motors, and he was the regional organiser for the BCSG way back in the early 70's, and I became good friends with him... I'm jumping the gun a little bit, so I don't want to forget any of these early memories because they really are gold dust.

As I told you, once the winter came round pike fishing was the way we went and we would often travel quite long distances to fish for pike in our holidays from school. A friend of mine, Alan Minns had a HA Viva van at the time, and how he ever got around in this thing I don't know as it was on its last legs when he bought it, but we would drive to Scotland and Wales regularly in this HA van. We went up to Wales and fished Lake Bala during the early holidays in the spring before the season would open on 16th June, and also up to Scotland to fish on Loch Lomond and Loch Ken. I remember one particular trip in 1972 when we drove up to Loch Ken to go pike fishing and were greeted by an awesome sight on one of the large peninsulas of land there overlooking the Loch. There was a large tent erected on this bit of land and on every available part of the point were rods set high up on bite alarms and rod rests. The first thing that I noticed was the size of the reels; they were Mitchell reels much like our Mitchell 300's but nearly three times the size. Everything was painted camouflage including the large tent, and there were four guys sleeping in this tent who we chatted to and arranged to meet in the local pub later that day. These four guys turned out to be British Carp Study Group members too from all over the country. I remember one guy was from Leicester, one guy was from Gloucester, and the other two were from around the London area somewhere but they'd all driven up to Loch Ken to fish for pike during the closed season, and they had the most amazing tackle that I had ever seen in my life. These guys actually told Alan and me about the carp baits they were using, which were these high nutritional mixes with eggs type of boilies that are used now. It wasn't that it was in one ear and out the other, but by this time we were catching quite consistently using sweetcorn for carp, which was an absolutely deadly bait in the 70's. I suppose we were not really willing to try these specials, and it wasn't until quite a few years later that I made my first boilies.

So having chatted to these guys over the space of two or three days about their carp fishing, the different lakes they were fishing up and down the country and these exotic baits, I went away with quite a lot of knowledge, which I was later to rely on.

My first double figure carp came on opening morning in 1970 fishing on

Another that fell to sweetcorn.

My last fish from Woburn Sands circa 1977.

22lb linear from the Airman around 1974.

Stanton Harcourt 1970.

A couple of shots of the Airman Pool at Henlow, Bedfordshire.

the Shovel Lake at Woburn Sands. I'd followed the approach of Big Frank who I'd seen fishing on there a couple of years before, but instead of using specials I was using sweetcorn. I had the tiniest little Arlesey bomb you could possible imagine on the line, a 1/8th of an ounce Arlesey bomb, which was hardly worth putting on there really. Fishing on one of the corner areas I baited along the left hand margin and dropped a couple of rods with the little yellow nuggets into my marginal spots. At around about 4am June 16th 1970, it rattled off, and it was my first double figure carp, a fish of 10lb 8oz. Unfortunately I never got any photographs of this carp but during that season I had quite a few doubles, I think about ten from Woburn Sands, mainly from the larger lake actually, all on sweet corn and all by fishing the margins. By casting two rod-lengths out you were in very deep water, but the marginal shelf was a fantastic place for sweetcorn in those early days.

Another gravel pit on the Vauxhall Angling Club ticket was Wyboston, also known as Hoveringham Gravel Pit. Armed with my deadly sweetcorn bait in 1972, I made quite a few visits to this lovely little pit (part of a golf course now, I believe). I began by fishing the entrance to a small backwater between two islands, and the first carp I landed weighed over 18lb, a good fish for the day. Little did I know that this fish was the largest in the lake and would go on to achieve weights of over 30lb in years to come. The lake held upwards of 50 carp I believe, and that first year I landed about a dozen, either on corn or floating crust.

The following year, I decided to swim out to one of the small islands and build a swim. There was just about enough room for my brolly camp, so I baited up with corn a few times and fished it opening week, ferrying my kit out to the island on top of a lilo. What a great adventure it was, all alone on my little island. I caught loads of carp, eight in fact on opening night, which I kept in two homemade carp sacks, four in each, and I photographed them all on the floor in the morning! What a kerfuffle, I can tell you. Carp fishing was still in its infancy, and no one had even thought of an unhooking mat let alone owned one. Grass was all we had – a far cry from today's luxury carp cradles where a newborn baby could sleep comfortably.

There were quite a few major changes toward the mid to late 70's. Of course the hair rig, Lenny Middleton's wonderful gift to carp anglers all over the world, became known to carp anglers everywhere. It was all kept very quiet when it first came out; in fact a number of lakes actually banned the hair rig before it was ever used. Duncan Kay was a big name in carp fishing at this time, and he was quick to ban the hair rig on his Mid Northants carp fisheries. I'm not sure quite what he thought was going to be so bad about the hair rig, but it was indeed banned. Boilies too became a lot more widely used. Fred Wilton's writings and other well-known carp anglers of the day began to put together the very first boilie baits.

I was working at Vauxhall at this time as a draftsman, and on one Saturday afternoon while I was working overtime, a guy came into the drawing office (bearing in mind this was January I believe and carp fishing as far as we knew it had all shut up shop) to say that he'd just come back that morning from taking his dog for a walk around Stanborough Lakes. Stanborough in Welwyn Garden City was a man made lake in a park; it had been dug in the early 70's and it had a butyl rubber lining, and it had been stocked with a large number of carp. I had actually fished Stanborough for a couple of seasons using luncheon meat and sausage meat as baits. Once again up to my old tricks, I would fish it mainly at night even though there was a night fishing ban on the lake. I actually got caught over there by Stuart Arnold who was a bailiff on the lake at the time and had a tackle shop in Welwyn Garden City. He was a big, flamboyant tackle dealer of the day and of course, up to no good as usual, Maylin and a couple of mates were down there after midnight pulling in the carp. Of course you could catch a lot more at night, and they were all on sausage meat and luncheon meat baits. Once again, we were using little bits of silver paper as indicators, and you would sit there with your hand over your rod with this thing twitching up and down for hours on end as the fish gradually whittled away the large lump of meat until they had virtually hooked themselves on a bit of exposed hook.

Anyway, this particular guy came into the drawing office and said he'd just been for a walk around there and watched a couple of guys catching some carp. I said, "Are you sure they were carp because it's very cold out there? I thought the lake would be frozen," and he said, "Well actually half the lake is frozen but they were up the other end. They're firing in these tiny little balls with a catapult that looks as though it's come from some science fiction movie." This was like a carrot dangling in front of a donkey to me, and I quickly packed away my pens and pencils, stood the drawing board upright, jumped in the car, and drove down to Stanborough. Sure enough, here were the ultra-cult carp anglers at the start of modern day carp fishing if you like, and I met the guys from the Carp Cellar for the first time.

The Carp Cellar was a shop in Watford; it was one of the first specialist, if not the first specialist carp shop in the country. I mean Alan Brown's was a specialist shop but it did all sorts of fishing – pike, salmon, everything, but the Carp Cellar was just carp, and it was run by Lloyd Bent. It was he and a few of his friends who had decided to pull off their Colne Valley waters that

20-pounder from the Airman.

(Left) Getting down and dirty at the Airman.
(Right) This is how it all began.

(Left) A Royalty barbel.
(Right) Linford Lakes pike.

Wyboston gravel pit, showing the entrance to the backwater and the little island I fished.

SPECIES: MIRROR CARP : DATE: 8TH JULY 1977: TIME: 11.35 P.M : WATER: WYBOSTON GRAVEL PITS.
WEIGHT: 6lB 2oz.
TACKLE: MITCHEL 300; 6oz CARP ROD; 8lB MAXIMA; ½TH oz ARLSEY BOMB; A.A SHOT;
SIZE 4 ALLCOCKS MODEL PERFECT SHORT SHANK HOOK.
BAIT : 2 NIBLETS OF BEJAM CUT CORN SWEETENED WITH SUGAR
TACTICS: AS ON 25TH JUNE 1977.

COMMENTS: FISH MADE 1 RUN WHEN FIRST HOOKED, BUT CAME IN QUITE EASILY,
IT WAS KEPT UNTIL MORNING WHEN IT WAS PHOTOGRAPHED & RETURNED.
2 PINTS OF CORN WAS PUT IN BEFORE STARTING, AND SECONDARY
FEED WAS PUT IN AFTER FISH WERE TAKEN.
WIND VERY STRONG, IN MY FACE. SLIGHT DRIZZLE. WARM WATER.

'Catch Data Card' for Wyboston in the seventies.

Biggest carp in the lake.

My setup – no buzzers and nothing matching.

Four carp per sack!

they had been fishing during the summer and go onto Stanborough for the winter. They had the hair rig, they had boilies, they had wrist rockets to fire the boilies out, and none of these three things had ever been seen on Stanborough before. The Colne Valley waters that they had pulled off were Savay, the Conservative Club and the Fisheries; three of the most awesome waters carp fishing history has ever known. This was long before the syndicate on Savay; these were Ruislip members, and I stood in amazement watching these three guys firing out these tiny balls and catching carp after carp.

One of the little balls came flying out of the catapult and landed in the grass close to me. The guy who was doing the fishing, his name was Jeff Rendall, one of the top carp anglers of the day and, well, still is to this day. He's a good friend of mine and I actually told him this story. Anyway, I searched around until I found it and sneakily stuck it in my pocket without telling him. I watched them fishing for a while with their boilies, which were all being made on the bank and dried out on a bedchair with a special cover on it like I'd never seen before. Afterwards I went home and tried to examine this ball to find out what on earth it was made out of. I called a couple of my close fishing friends, Simon Day and Gary Bearman and we all looked at this ball in amazement. What it actually was, as I found out from Jeff some years later, was liquidised squid and semolina. They were fishing two baits that week; one rod on liquidised squid and semolina with a fish essence and the other one on a high nutrient value milk protein with an orange colour and orange flavour. You can imagine the things that we came up with trying to imitate these balls.

In fact around about this time I began writing to Duncan Kay. At this point I had caught quite a number of 20lb carp from Arlesey Lake, mostly on sweetcorn or floating crust. Duncan Kay was the bait guru of the time, and I asked him as a young teenager whether he could help me out with a few bait recipes and one or two places that I might go to catch a 30lb carp. Slowly the jigsaw was put together; Duncan Kay gave me a few tips, and he actually gave me a list of waters which contained carp to 30lb. I'd really like to dig these old letters out, as I haven't thrown them away, and they must be within all my piles of junk somewhere. The waters included Billing Aquadrome, the River Ouse, Arlesey Lake and his own Mid Northants carp fishery, and at the end of the letter he said, "When you've caught all these," because there was only one in each lake, "Write to me again and I'll give you a list of some even harder ones to catch," which really made me laugh at the time.

But anyway, I had Arlesey Lake, and I had Stanborough, which contained a lot of small single and double figure carp and the odd 20. There was a similar lake actually up the road at Fairlands Valley in Stevenage, which in hindsight, I don't think I actually fished until around about 1980 if my memory serves me right – I'm a little bit rusty on the exact years to be honest. Anyway, we set about formulating our own boilies, and the first ones weren't far away from the liquidised squid – we actually used liquidised sardines from a tin. Instead of using semolina we used breakfast cereal as a binder, and eggs, and boiled them, but they never really went hard; they were a bit squidgy. What with the writing of Fred Wilton, which was opened up to me through my involvement at that time with Len and the various recipes from Duncan Kay, we soon came up with our high nutritional value bait, which was not far off the HMV baits of today, containing all the same type of milk proteins, casein, lactalbumin, calcium caseinate, semolina, ground rice, that type of thing. There were nowhere near the amount of flavours and additives around. Kevin Nash actually was one of the first to have a range of flavours, and they were called Karp Krave, all in glass bottles, and Alan Brown sold these as did The Carp Cellar in Watford. Richworth was in its infancy, and two regular carp anglers who used the shop and also fished Savay in the early days, Malcolm Winkworth and Clive Dietrich, came up with the first commercial frozen boilies.

But once again I'm jumping the gun a little bit here, so let's go back to those early days of Stanborough. Once I got my ticket back after my night fishing exploits, I was banned for a season, but got my ticket back the next year and went on to catch hundreds of carp from Stanborough, including the odd 20lb'er. I became more friendly with Len Gurd who would kindly take me to the BCSG meetings that were being held around the country. Len would hold the BCSG meetings in Dunstable, and Duncan Kay would hold the BCSG meetings in Northants, and Len asked me if I would like to run the recently formed Carp Anglers Association, CAA, for Bedfordshire, Hertfordshire, Buckinghamshire and Oxford, which I loved to do. On a monthly basis I would hire a hall in Dunstable, write a letter to about 200-300 members in that area and invite them along to watch a slide show and be generally entertained by speakers, along with a tackle stand and bait stand. There were very few people that had tackle and bait stands at the time, but Geoff Kemp was a young lad who had just started up selling bait, and another young lad who had just started up selling tackle was Kevin Nash, and both of these guys would turn up in their little vans. They had nobody working for them at all; they were one-man bands and put on a little display of their wares.

At the time, Kevin only sold his flavours, a carp sack, a weigh sling and

My early equipment.

Cool shirt, hey?

(Left) A Wyboston linear.
(Right) Floating crust did the job.

Stanborough.

One from the 'Out of Bounds'.

One rod and all this to put up with.

Boilie-caught carp.

maybe a little carryall or something, but very, very little, and Jeff had a range of powders and flavours. I would invite these guys regularly to come along and watch the slide shows of the time. These were put on by anglers such as John Baker, Kevin Maddocks, and Alan Downey. Now there's a name from the past, Alan Downey, you never hear about him any more. He was a very good and eccentric angler who fished Wormleybury and places around the Hertford area, Broxbourne etc, and he had a fantastic slide show, which we watched every year. Bruce Ashby had made a movie about catching a couple of 30lb carp with a colleague of his, Roy Johnson, and I saw the movie on a couple of occasions in those early days, on 8mm film reel, maybe in the early 70's. It was actually at one of these BCSG meetings, after having three or four pints of beer, that I was stopped by the police on the way home, breathalysed, and lost my licence for a year. I know that that was 1973, so that's when I saw Bruce's film that particular night. What a nightmare.

The BCSG would also have an annual conference, which was held either at Hatfield Polytechnic or the London School of Economics if my memory serves me right, and the great anglers of the day: Bob Morris, Jack Simpson, and Kevin again, would all put on slide shows and talks. It was an amazing time because this was all brand new; there weren't all the magazines we have today; the only carp magazines that was out there was firstly The Carp, the BCSG magazine, and that was highly exclusive. Hardly anybody ever got in the BCSG, and I'll tell you about my exploits trying to get in the BCSG in a moment. Then there was the CAA magazine, which was out I think four times a year, or something like that. The Carp Society didn't exist until 1980 so these were the carp fishing magazines of the time, and there was nothing else to read. You couldn't wait until one of these publications came out, and you would read it from cover to cover, 20 or 30 times, trying to digest every little bit of information from all these ultra-secret guys around the country, all coming together as one to discuss their secrets and pool their knowledge.

The BCSG meetings in the Bedfordshire area were also a little bit different to the meetings of today, as we would have strippers. We would always have two or three girls come along and end up doing an exotic dancing routine, usually ending up with a couple of guys on the floor with them at the end. What would carp anglers think of that today I wonder? Well, it depends where you stand I suppose, but you know, a lot of people didn't like Peter Mohan and thought that he was the wrong person for the job, but he was a very open-minded guy, and he didn't want carp fishing to get political. But there was an element of people out there who had been refused entry to the BCSG and did want to get political, and it was some of these who formed the Carp Society in 1980. Once again, its first meeting was in Dunstable.

Anyway, I applied for the BCSG in the late 70's and Peter, who didn't know me well at that time, asked me to make a list of all the double figure carp that I had caught in the preceding three seasons. Of course by fishing waters like Stanborough, catching 100 double figure carp in a season was fairly commonplace, and after sending my first application back, he wrote back with a very snooty letter saying that he basically didn't believe me. I had caught more carp this season than the whole of the rest of the BCSG put together, which made me laugh. The following season I applied again and once again I think I'd caught something like 140 carp over double figures, mainly from Stanborough and those well-stocked waters around my area, and several 20lb'ers as well. I didn't catch my first 30lb carp until I believe 1981 and we'll get to that in a moment. But anyway, I was turned down twice by Peter for the BCSG. Later on, I think it was in 1983 when I wrote Tiger Bay, which was published by Kevin Maddocks, a very great friend of Peter's, Peter actually apologised to me saying that he now realised that what I'd said I'd caught was true. I think I'd caught something like 17 30lb'ers, which again was pretty much unheard of for the day. I was speaking to him at BK Publishers up at Henlow, and he said, "I'll make you a life member of the BCSG to make up for it." Unfortunately he doesn't have much to do with the BCSG any more, and I never ever did receive a membership for the BCSG. I so dearly wanted one of those little badges of the carp with the letters BCSG on there and my magazines each year, but I never did get to be a member. Even to this day I'm not a member of the BCSG, although I'm sure most of the members think I probably am.

So after writing to Duncan Kay on numerous occasions about these waters which contained carp over 30lb, one of the waters which he mentioned to me was a lake known as the Banjo Lake at Stanstead Abbotts in Hertfordshire. In the early 70's, I went on a couple of recce trips over there to look around this Banjo and its notorious 30lb'er known as Nelson, a carp with one eye obviously. On applying to Leisure Sport, when Jack Ashford was in control, I was unfortunately told that the venue was full and that I should apply again next year. Another water, although just a little bit too far afield for me to travel to, which was in the headlines at that time was Darenth and there and the Banjo Lake, although not the main lake, seemed to be the places, certainly on Leisure Sports tickets anyway, where carp fishing was growing in leaps and bounds. Now Darenth has been massively written about, but I have never even walked on its banks I've got to say, as Stanstead Abbotts was nearer. I told Duncan Kay that I intended to fish Stanstead Abbotts, and then wrote to him some weeks later to say that I unfortunately I couldn't get in, as the venue was fully subscribed. Then Duncan did the most wonderful thing, as Jack Ashford was a friend of his. He approached Jack directly and managed to get a ticket for me, and do you know, I'm ashamed to say that I never even went to the venue. It wasn't until probably 20 or so years later that I ventured up to Stanstead Abbotts one September day and cast a boilie into the main lake, only to catch the biggest fish in the venue, which even to this day is known as Maylin's Fish, a truly wonderful and beautiful looking carp from this fantastic venue.

20lb'ers were the target that we all wanted to achieve, and Arlesey Lake had given me quite a few in those early days by fishing floating crust and corn. But now at the end of the 70's and the beginning of the 80's, armed with the first carbon fibre rods, the Sportex 2¼lb blank, which became the first Kevin Maddocks carp rod marketed by Simpsons of Turnford, and the new reels, the ultra-cult reels of the time, the Abu Cardinal 55, 155, 57 and 157, we felt like we had the gear and the bait to go and catch 20lb carp or even bigger by design. Thinking back to my early purchase of these

Action at Fairlands.

22 pounder from Stanborough.

Fairlands 21 pounder – the lake's first 20.

One in the snow from '5 Springs'.

Complete with backdrop!

The D/E lake divide at Waveney Valley.

'The Back' of 'D' Lake.

expensive carp fishing items, I actually got myself my first credit card just so that I could go over to the Carp Cellar and buy a pair of Sportex 11ft 2¼'s and Abu Cardinal reels, and I went for the larger size, the 57 size, which were actually stolen from me up on the Copse Lake at Yateley some years later when I had all my tackle nicked, but I digress again.

Yeah, going down to the Carp Cellar in Watford with my credit card in my hand, I'd loaded it up with rods, reels, bite indicators, the lot, and an instant carp angler of 1978, if you like, was born. Great memories – we suddenly found that we could cast over 50yds, which was nice, and we wanted to get onto some venues that held carp in excess of 30lbs. Around about this time Savay hit the headlines. It had been taken over by the syndicate, but the Ruislip Club still had exclusivity to some of the banks, and it was being run by Graham Rowles of Redland Aggregates, and Peter

Fairlands carp.

Broxup was a bailiff at the time. There were articles on Savay in the angling papers with people saying how ridiculous it was that there were more than one 30lb'er in these venues, and how easy it was going to make it for everybody to catch multiple catches of 30lb'ers as there were shoals of them swimming around in Savay. This would have been around about 1980 I believe, as it was the following season that Andy Little went on there and caught, which was a record at the time, 13 30's in a season, shoulder to shoulder for the first time with the best carp anglers in the country namely Kevin Maddocks, Rod Hutchinson, Lenny Middleton etc.

The other venue that we'd heard about was the Waveney Valley complex in Norfolk. At the time I believe the complex of ten or 12 lakes had three 30lb'ers to its name. G Lake had a well known carp called Gertie, whereas C and D Lake, two lakes joined by a channel of water, also had two 30lb'ers, one in each if you like, or two in the pair. These were the awesome Waveney Leather, one of the only 30lb leathers in the country, and a beautiful mirror known as Big Scale. So it was in 1981 that I made my first trip up to Waveney. I fished C Lake for the first few days of my holiday, and there were quite a few things going on a Waveney that I hadn't seen elsewhere, for instance 'sponging up' as it was known.

I met a guy who was fishing on D Lake called Alan Taylor who later became a very famous carp angler and was heavily involved with Kevin Maddocks in his videos of the day. Alan had wedged a large bung of sponge in his butt ring to hold the line tight. We had open bale arms at the time; the line clip had been invented, although there wasn't a commercially made one at the time and everything had to be homemade. A small piece of old glass or carbon fibre fishing rod whipped down by the butt was all that you needed, but up here they realised the benefits of a continued tension when the fish was pulling line from the spool. Of course once the line came out of the line clip on an open bale arm, the line just fell and sprung out all over the place, whereas with a bung of foam in the butt ring, everything was kept under tension. For some reason, people hadn't thought that just to release the spool slightly would give you that same tension, and of course today we all take it for granted that just loosening the spool or a bait runner is all you need just to keep that tension there, but it's all a learning curve, and as I say, people just hadn't really put two and two together.

Chapter 1
The big League — The Search for Known Waters

"They were the matt black brigade and everything was top secret, hush hush, even I was sworn to secrecy."

Going up to Waveney Valley Lakes that first time in 1982 was, I suppose, my introduction to the 'Big League'. Although I'd fished quite a few waters in the last 12 years including Woburn Sands, Wyboston gravel pits, Stanborough Lake, Fairlands Valley Lake and the Vauxhall waters, Tingrith Manor and the Oxford water Stanton Harcourt and of course Arlesey, at this point I hadn't really fished any known waters. By known waters I mean waters that had received a lot of publicity in recent years; waters where the big carp anglers of the day would go and fish. These were waters such as Redmire Pool, Ashlea Pool and Billing Aquadrome to name a few – waters that had been well written about over the years. There had been films made too; I remember an excellent film at one of the early BCSG annual conferences in London. It was made down at Ashlea Pool featuring a guy called Vic Gillings, who is unfortunately dead now. The effort that these guys put in to catch these fish was mindblowing, along with the knowledge that they had of baits and successful rigs of the day.

I suppose Arlesey Lake was the best known in my area; at that time in the late 70's and early 80's it contained a 30lb carp, called the Big Girl. I never saw it on the bank; it died before I actually fished there, or maybe the first year I fished there. There were some quite good anglers fishing the lake at the time; a couple of BCSG guys who had written articles about waters in the area. I can't for the life of me think of the surname of a guy who I spent quite a lot of time with round about 1980 on the lake. His first name was Alan; I can't remember his surname, but he'd written a few articles in the old BCSG magazines, and knew his stuff. Also, of course, a young Dave Thorpe lived local to the lake. Dave was a good angler, very, very competitive, and I might even say quite a jealous angler too. He didn't handle other people catching fish very well and would often end up in a big strop if someone else was catching a lot, but he certainly caught more than his fair share. I mean this guy virtually lived at Arlesey in those first few years of the 80's. He went on to Elstow from Arlesey at a time when there were very few 20lb'ers in there, and no 30's at all. He certainly could never have dreamt how the lake would be today with its fair number of 40's, but I remember he went on there and caught 100 doubles in a season, which was a massive achievement for that time.

Dave was a good surface angler as well. I remember he made this controller, which looked like a hand grenade. It was a huge ball of polystyrene with a 2oz lead in the middle, and it was like a brick when it hit the water, but he certainly nailed some fish off the top with it. Arlesey was an exceptional water for surface fishing; a water that I was actually fishing at this time, but hadn't fished for a couple of years, and my first 20lb'ers all came from Arlesey in the late 70's. Redmire was a syndicate, Ashlea Pool was a syndicate, and Billing Aquadrome, well, I can't really remember, but it was certainly a tall order to catch a fish out of there. It was one of the waters that Duncan Kaye had written to me about, and said that there was a 30lb'er in there, and that it was a water that perhaps I should have a look at if I wanted to catch a 30, which I did at this time. But Waveney Valley of course was a water that was accessible to everybody – a day ticket venue with about eight lakes.

I remember arriving at the venue; three of us went on that first trip, and we really wanted to get on D Lake, which was the one that seemed to have the bigger fish – the one where the serious anglers concentrated their efforts. There were two 30lb'ers at the time – a fish called Big Scale, a mirror of around about 31-32lb I think, and the Leather, one of only about three leather carp in the country that went over 30lbs that were known about at the time, or that were written about, let's say. Savay ended up having a couple of carp in there that went over 30lbs, but other than that, there was Heather the Leather at 30lb down in the Car Park Lake and another one up in the north, on a water I remember Tim Paisley used to fish. Of course that fish died; I can't remember the name of it now, but there were two 30's in there, and quite a head of 20lbers.

D Lake was joined to E Lake by a small channel of water, although I think the fish were usually resident in D. The Leather and Big Scale had been caught out of E Lake, but rarely compared to the number of times they were caught out of D, which was the lake they liked to be in for obvious reasons, as it was bigger. The fish over there were highly pressured for the time, and took shelter under the undercut banks on the far side during the daytime. It was virtually impossible to get a bite unless you were actually clipping the hawthorns and brambles with your lead over to what they called 'The Back'.

The swims were numbered, with number 1 being right on the gap, on the channel between D and E. The angler in Swim 1 would fish up the spur of land, which divided the two lakes. In Swim 2, he had a bit more choice; he could actually fish right up into the top corner where the spur of land joined The Back with his right hand rod, and actually put his left hand rod on the bramble bushes and hawthorns to the left of that corner. Swim 3 was pole position really I think, and the swim that I was able to fish the following year and catch the Leather from funnily enough, but we will get to that. Swim 3 offered you a nice choice of features on the far margin. I think there were only about five or six swims on D Lake and less on E Lake – they were quite small lakes. But the thing was, you could only really fish one bank. On most lakes you could fish on all four banks, but on this lake you only had the one bank, and you fished as far away from you as you possibly could.

I think we'd read about it in the Angling Times; I think they were advertising the fishing in there, but for whatever reason we made our minds up to go. Me and two guys that I worked with at Vauxhall who worked down in the prototype modelling section, Simon Day and his apprentice (who we only ever referred to as 'Prentice'). He lost the A off the front, and was never actually called by his real name. He was the dogsbody I suppose; he would carry the gear, make the tea, do the washing up, tidy the swims, just for the pleasure of being in Simon's company, and being his apprentice at Vauxhall. Simon was a very skilled worker, and Prentice was learning his trade from Simon and sort of followed him around like a little lap dog. The three of us decided to go up to Waveney; we couldn't get on D Lake, but E Lake was empty, and the three of us virtually filled it. I think there were four swims actually, but we took the first swims past the entrance into D Lake.

We tossed a coin, and I won the toss and took the left hand side of the swim, with Simon next to me and Prentice to his right. We fished there that first weekend, and it was quite eventful. There were loads of things going on in carp fishing at this time, bait-wise, the first commercial boilies were available. We were making our own boilies by this time but the first commercial ones had actually hit the market. I don't know whether anyone reading this will remember them, but they were actually in a bubble pack on a strip, and you would tear off how many boilies you wanted at the shop and buy them. It sounds unbelievable I know but they were packaged on a long strip and bubble-wrapped individually so you would go in a say, "Can I buy six boilies?" and they would tear six off the end of this roll. I can't remember the name of them, but they may have been by Gerry Savage, I'm not sure.

Gerry Savage was a well-known angler of the day; in fact he'd probably been around for ten years before this and brought out his own high nutritional value base mix, which was, I believe, only Phillips yeast mix. Yeast mix was a very, very popular attractor at the time, but it's something that has virtually disappeared from carp fishing these days. I may very well have just mentioned something that could certainly put some more fish on the bank for people. It's funny how these things have a popularity lifespan, and then suddenly no one uses them any more, but yeast was major part of everyone's bait at that time; that very distinctive smell and taste, and fish loved it. It's virtually overlooked these days in carp fishing baits, but at the time, Gerry Savage had his high protein bait out in tubs. You could buy these little tubs with probably about a pound of base mix in there, with an orange seal around it. I remember seeing them stacked up in the tackle shops of the

Prentice and me, set up on E Lake, 1982.

(Left) 25lb 3oz mirror on a side-hooked boilie, from E Lake.
(Above) Biggin Lakes permit 1983.

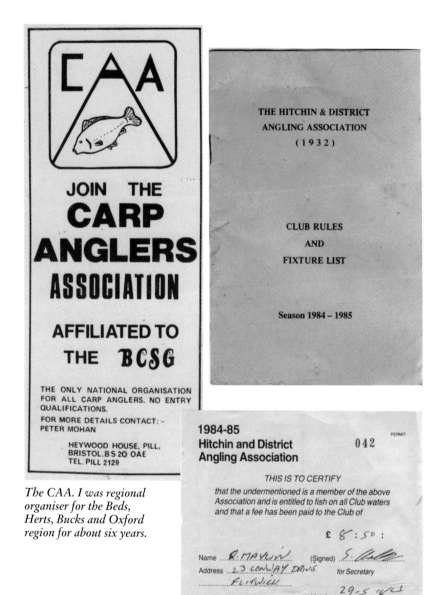

The CAA. I was regional organiser for the Beds, Herts, Bucks and Oxford region for about six years.

Hitchin & District were the controlling club for Arlesey in the early eighties.

Fairlands Valley setup, early eighties.

A very picturesque Biggin Lake. I only fished it a couple of times but caught a few stunning scaly carp.

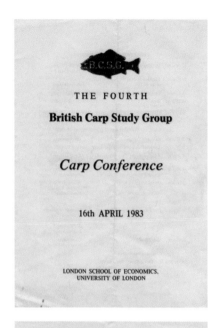

THE FOURTH

British Carp Study Group

Carp Conference

16th APRIL 1983

LONDON SCHOOL OF ECONOMICS,
UNIVERSITY OF LONDON

CONFERENCE PROGRAMME

11.00 a.m.	Opening of Conference	*BCSG Chairman, Peter Frost*
11.05 a.m.	Conference Organisation and History of the BCSG	*Peter Mohan*
11.15 a.m.	Tackle—Facts, Fancies and Folklore	*Jim Gibbinson*
12.15 p.m.	Reels	*Barrie Welham*
1.00 p.m.	LUNCH TACKLE SHOW BAR	
	SALE OF RAFFLE TICKETS	
	SALE OF FOURTH BCSG BOOK (BCSG STAND)	
2.45 p.m.	Baits and Things	*Geoff Kemp*
3.30 p.m.	Are you Fishing in the Right Spot?	*Alan Downie*
4.00 p.m.	A Decade in the Carp Fishing of . . .	*Keith Gillings/ Kevin Maddocks*
4.30 p.m.	The Wrong End of the Stick	*Bruce Ashby/ Bob James*
5.00 p.m.	On the Surface	*Movie film featuring Duncan Kay and Peter Mohan*
5.20 p.m.	TEA	
6.00 p.m.	Discussion—Sacks or Keepnets?	*'Sacker' Maddocks, 'Keepnet' Kay, Jim Gibbinson, Del Romang, Roger Emmet*
6.45 p.m.	Slide Show	*Chad Valley Specimen Group*
	Closing of Conference	
7.45 to 10 p.m.	Tackle Show Bar Raffle	
	Cafeteria open for meals until 9 p.m.	

The British Carp Study Group Conferences were the world's first carp
conferences. This Fourth BCSG Conference is attended by around 550
delegates, and was organised for the BCSG by:

Peter Mohan	*Conference Chairman*
Kevin Maddocks	*Tackle Show Manager*
John Baker	*Photography and Technical*
David Albone	*Displays*
Len Gurd	*BCSG Stand*
Dave Powell	*Raffle*
Keith Gillings	
Ron Middleton	
Alan Smith	*Stewards*
Roger Emmet	
Lee Jackson	
Bob Davis	
Rob Maylin	*CAA Stand*
David Brown	*Signwriting*
Brenda Maddocks	*Reception*
Tina Kemp	

The Organisers wish to thank all those who have contributed in any way
to the success of this Fourth BCSG Conference.

TACKLE SHOW, ROOMS 1, 2 and 3

Opening Times: 1 p.m. to 2.45 p.m.; 7.45 p.m. to 10 p.m.

Exhibitors:

Veals of Bristol	Chris Brown Rods
The Tackle Carrier	Partridge of Redditch
Duncan Kay's Angling Services	Andy Barker Fishing Tackle
Kent Angling	Penge Angling Supplies
Key Angling Supplies	Anglers' Co-operative Association
Simpson's of Turnford	Anglemark
Daiwa	Alan Brown of Hitchin
Leeda Mitchell Service Stand	D.A.M. Tackle
Geoff Kemp Baits	Tackle Up
Robin West Slide Show	H. Steade & Sons
Happy Hooker Products	Strentex Fabrics
Richworth Ltd	Brian Mills Carvings & Drawings
Dave Barnes Umbrella Tents	Nicholson & Thorpe Angling
Pro' Bait	Supplies
Bruce Ashby Rods	PKF Engineering Ltd
North Western Blanks	Terry Eustace Tackle
Bamford Optonic Conversions	Bob Morris
British Carp Study Group	Anglebooks
Carp Anglers' Association	Fox International Ltd

B.C.S.G. Carp Conference programme 1983. The highlight of the show was a debate between 'Sacker' Maddocks and 'Keepnet' Kay about which was best for retaining carp.

day; the very first commercial carp bait that you could buy, and then these boilies came along in the bubble strip. I'm not sure whether that was him or not, but it may well have been.

On site at Waveney there was a tackle shop. I haven't been up there for 30 years so, and whether that's still there or not, I don't know. But there was this little shop up there, and on the wall were pictures of guys with big smiles on their faces with some of the Waveney fish. There were quite a few pictures of different people with the Leather, and different people with Big Scale. There was another well-known 30 in G Lake called Gertie, Gertie the Thirty, and there were pictures of that too. That fish, if I remember rightly, used to come out quite a few times a year – we're talking maybe 15-20 times – out of G Lake. Then there was another one, I believe, in C Lake, which was just to the left of D as you looked out of the shop window, and also a lake that I was going to fish the following year.

So we bought our tickets, and we'd got our own boilies that we had made. In fact I'm going to tell you about mine, because mine became a bit of a legend. Another thing that was going on of course with carp fishing at this time was the explosion of rig design. Lenny Middleton's hair rig had been divulged to those in the know around about 1980, and obviously we'd got on that as well fairly quickly, and quite a number of people were using it up at Waveney. When we got there we were surprised at how many people were using it. Alan Taylor was fishing on D Lake in Swim 3, and he was using pop-ups with some high density foam sponge rammed into the butt ring to give a constant drag.

We were very clued-up anglers for the time, but we weren't convinced that the old predecessor of the hair rig, side hooking, had had its day completely. We caught so many fish side hooking our baits – just using quite a large hook and burying the shank within the boilie, but leaving the whole bend and very, very sharp point sticking out. It was like a claw sticking out of the side of the bait, and we fished it on a fairly short link with a fixed lead, which accounted for hundreds of carp for me in 1980 and 1981.

We would fish one bait side hooked and one on a hair rig. On the hair rigs of the day, the hair could be anything from an inch minimum to 3 or 4ins long. It sounds extraordinary today to think of using a hair rig that long, as most of my hairs these days are no more than a quarter of an inch long. I know some people these days do use long hairs and still catch fish, and we used to catch fish on long hairs, don't get me wrong. I went through the whole scenario of hair rig fishing when I first heard about it, and actually used 6in long hairs of half a pound breaking strain line tied to the bend of the hook, and then a 2ft or 2ft 6in hooklink. There was plenty of movement in it, because obviously if they're sucking the boilie in you want the hook to follow on. They've got to suck the boilie right back to the throat teeth, and they're virtually crapping it out, let alone swallowing it, before the hook is in the mouth, but it still caught fish.

I think we were using around about an inch for hair length. Just about everybody either tied the hair off the bend or off the shank in those days. It was a year or so later that tying them through the eye became the norm. Everybody used to use a very fine hair when it first came out but it didn't take us long to realise that you could simply pass the remaining tail of your hooklink material through the eye and put a loop on it and pull your bait onto the loop, and it would be just as effective as tying this length of half a pound or one pound breaking strain line separately to the hook.

So it was an exciting time; it really was. I hadn't totally finished with Arlesey; in fact I fished Arlesey right up until about 1983, or I think it may have been 1984, but 1983 was the last proper year that I fished on there. I had come up with a boilie mix, a pop-up mix to use for the next 15 years on dozens of waters and it outfished anybody I fished up against; it really was the ultimate bait. There was a time when I first started the magazine in 1991 that I actually thought about marketing these pop-ups as guaranteed fish catchers, and just selling them in packets of six because you'd catch six carp on them, and I'm sure you would to this day. I used to buy my bait ingredients from a chap called Geoff Kemp, who had one of the first bait companies that you could buy ingredients from. He and Duncan Kay were the early ones; the Carp Cellar in Watford became synonymous with Richworth, but also sold bait ingredients.

All the proper carp anglers of the day would make their own bait. They pooh-poohed the mass manufactured commercial boilie, which was going to be, and still is, very, very popular, as most people buy readymade boilies these days. Our lives are so hectic and time is so precious these days, we just haven't got the time to sit for hours every night rolling bait, but in those days, bait was the be-all and end-all – if you had a good bait you kept it secret and you made your own bait religiously and carefully every night.

We had a lot of ideas about what the carp could actually detect and how acute their senses were. If you have ever read Jack Hilton's Quest for Carp, you'll no doubt recall the fact that when he put his bait on, he made sure that his hands smelled the same every time. He was a smoker so there was this slight tinge of nicotine, and for consistency, when putting out bait, baiting up or putting bait on the hook, he would make sure that his hands smelt identical each time. He was convinced in those early days that the carp would know the difference. If he'd been peeling an orange or something before putting his bait on, then the fish wouldn't eat it, so everything had to be the same. We know these days though that it's not so important… Well, none of us would argue that filling the car up with petrol and getting it all over your hands on the way to the lake would not be an ideal way to start the session. To put boilies on with petrol on your fingers, or after you've just opened a rusty old padlock on a gate without washing your hands in the lake, certainly could be detrimental to your captures. Even to this day, I still wash as soon as I get to the lake; I wash my hands in the mud and the gravel at the bottom of the lake so that most of the smells of modern day living and chemicals etc are taken out of my hands, and they just smell of the lakebed.

So I would purchase my bait ingredients from Geoff Kemp, as no tackle shops in my area sold bait ingredients. In fact the only one I knew of in the south of England was the Carp Cellar in Watford. Now the Carp Cellar was an underground cellar in a shop called the Tackle Carrier actually in Watford where Lloyd Bent and several other carp anglers worked. These guys were fishing the Cons, the Fisheries and Savay in the late 70's and early 80's and were well clued up bait-wise. I used to call Geoff before our annual BCSG or Carp Anglers Association meetings early in the year, in the closed season, and we would have a meeting, usually at Dunstable in the later years. It had been at the London School of Economics at Hatfield University, but was held quite a few times up at Dunstable in the Queensway Hall.

So I'd give him a call with my order and then I would purchase flavours from him and ingredients which included casein, lactalbumin in various forms, caseinates, calcium caseinate and soya isolate, which are high protein powders used in the food industry. They are food fit for human consumption, and you had to be very careful when buying casein that it wasn't the industrial casein that was used for glue making, which was called inedible casein – you had to purchase the edible casein. Casein was the ingredient that made your bait go very hard, as did egg albumin, but casein came in various degrees of coarsenesses – the granules would vary. You could have a very fine, high number; a 100-mesh casein would be a very fine casein, whereas a 30-mesh casein would be very coarse. It paid to have a variety of ingredients, a spectrum that covered the whole aspect of palatability. What you were trying to create with a high nutritional value bait was to make the carp feel good when they ate it – to make them want to come back for more. You wanted to give them more than natural food in the way of nutrition, so that in the end you educated the fish to eat that bait to the exclusion of anything else.

A very important part of the bait, other than the powdered ingredients

Duncan Kay's Angling Services

"Cyprinus Carpio", 15 Manor Way, Higham Ferrers, Northants.
Telephone Rushden 4395

V.A.T. Reg. No. 336 1999 27

Early letter from Duncan Kay. He and I would correspond about bait and where I could catch a 30!

Stanborough around 1980.

Some of my hundreds of Stanborough carp from the early eighties.

Len Gurd cartoon from 1983. Len and I worked at Vauxhall Motors and used to talk about carp fishing all day instead of working!

Another carp from Stanborough in the early eighties.

One of three 20's in a day from Arlesey in 1980 on floating crust

Excerpt from my carp log 1981-82 season describing the capture of a 14lb 15oz common.

that went into it, was the liquid ingredients and attractors. Sweeteners were something that came out in the early 80's, and it soon became obvious that a sweet bait was very palatable at the time; it was something that fish hadn't really come across. In the early days, carp anglers would put honey in their baits, but we soon found that adding a variety of sweeteners – a little lactose, the milk sugar, and a little fructose, the fruit sugar, would excite the taste buds of the fish. Vitamins were something important to add to the bait too. People these days realise the importance of taking vitamins to sustain health, to give you that feel good factor, and this is the thing we were trying to do with the baits – to give the carp that feel good factor when they ate them, so vitamins were an important part of the make-up of the bait. We would use milk type vitamin derivatives in the form of Equivite milk pellets, which were vitamin pellets for horses basically, but fish loved them. You could also purchase ingredients such as Vitamilo, and normal vitamin supplements that you could purchase from the health food shops. Bear in mind we're talking about 1981 here, or probably 1980 when I first came out with this bait, so even by today's standards it's pretty high tech.

Other ingredients that I found I didn't tell anyone about until around about 1985 when I wrote my first book, Tiger Bay. Up until that point I hadn't told anybody any of the baits that I was using, but there's quite a comprehensive bait section in Tiger Bay if you've ever read it. Even today people tell me that it was their reference, and it still is a good reference today for what ingredients are all about. But a couple of things that I found, I'd never heard or seen anybody use, at least not for years and years after. One of them was green-lipped mussel, which was a powder that had been compressed into a lozenge shape. They were very expensive, but you could get them in the health food shop in big brown bottles for about £10 a bottle, and I would crush these down and put them into the bait. No one, not even Rod Hutchinson, John Baker or Geoff Kemp or any of those who were the bait gurus of the time had never heard of anyone using it. Seaweed was another ingredient that I found – kelp – and no one had used it up to that point. Then there was corn steep liquor, another ingredient that I introduced into my bait. I did find some guys down in Essex who were using it, and I hadn't told them about it, so they'd come up with it themselves. So as you can see, the bait that I was using was already building into a bait, which, even now, 30 years later, would stand up against anything out there on the shelves.

When it came to flavours, I was very much into natural flavours, and very much into fish and meat flavours right from day one. This again went totally against what most people were doing at the time. Most people who were making their own baits had followed the writings of the time; Kevin Maddocks had written quite a bit on bait and he was a big cream and toffee and sweet confectionery type bait maker, as were John Baker and Geoff Kemp. Rod favoured this type of flavour as well with his maple creams, although he did bring out a seafood blend some years later, which was available as a boilie and a flavour, and that was an excellent bait, which caught me quite a few fish later on. But the flavours I used, I purchased from a variety of sources because nowhere did them all, and I wanted to cover every single taste scenario possible.

So I actually purchased salmon oil in two different forms; Alasalar stood for Atlantic salmon, and that could be purchased from the Carp Cellar in Watford. I didn't get hold of salmon oil as we use it today until around about 1984, and I purchased that from John Baker who didn't have a bait company at the time, but he was, or so he reliably informed me, a food broker, and dealt with a big flavour company, which I think might have been Rayners. He turned up at Savay around about 1984 with a load of litre bottles of this extraordinary salmon oil in the back of his car, and I had a couple of bottles of that. It drove the cats wild in my house; I was living in Flitwick at the time, and just opening the bottle would send them up the wall. I then combined this with some natural fish flavours from a variety of different fish.

Kevin Nash had a range of flavours out called Karp Krave in glass bottles, and I purchased these from Alan Browns at Hitchin, and he did pilchard and mackerel and cod. There was also a tackle manufacturer that sold fish oils in little bottles, which were for pike fishing. They came in a little flat bottle with square flat edges and a green label on it; it may have been Efgeeco, and these I purchased from Wilds. I ended up with about 20 different liquid attractors, of which some were oil based and some were synthetic, based on a chemical base. The oil ones had to be emulsified to make them water friendly, and I did this with lecithin, which is again from the health food shop, and I'd never seen it in any fishing baits up until that point.

It was an amazing bait that I created – I made pop-ups with it, and I did something very, very different with the pop-ups, something that I have never ever told anybody about, not even my closest fishing friends. I've written about making pop-ups in my books, but in the early books I tell you to put them on cocktail sticks so there's a hole already in there, and then microwave them. In my later writings, I realised the importance of overnight buoyancy, making them with cork balls, drying them down, and introducing lots of goodness into them, sense appeals etc. Yes I've written about that, but I have never ever told anybody how I made my little pop-ups, which were nicknamed The Legends. The guys who fished with me at the time – Steve Alcott, Dave Wibley, Martin Locke, and others hammered me and hammered me for information about the bait and how I had made it, because everywhere we went it caught 20 times as much as anybody else. I started using it up on Waveney and Arlesey, and took it to the Mid-Northants carp fishery, Duncan Kaye's water, and caught the biggest fish in there.

It would catch the biggest ones straight away, and it was instant at Savay. I had a bite the first day I was down there, the first day on day ticket at Savay. Imagine getting a bite and the syndicate people just looking at you and thinking, who the hell is that Noddy who's just had a bite straight away? And so it went on; the list of waters is endless – the Waltonians, Fox Pool, Harefield. It was an extraordinary catcher at Harefield. I'm sure some of you have seen the Harefield Haulin' videos – those little orange baits that I fished... I never put them out as free offerings for some reason, well they may have worked, and I think I did try sometimes, but I just didn't need to. It didn't matter what the free offerings were; you could just pile a load of hemp or a load of any sort of boilies you liked in as free offerings, but the first bait that would be eaten as the fish came into the swim were those little orange ones that I made, those Legends. We went to Withy Pool for the day, and it was a hard water at that time, when Kevin Maddocks had it, and I caught a fish on the first day on them, which would leave people shaking their heads. People offered me £5, and I'm talking about in the 80's, £5 a boilie, not a word of lie.

When I was fishing with them down at Stanborough, people would come along and say, "Sell me a boilie... I'll give you a fiver for one pop-up." I probably could have made a fortune out of them, but I never actually got round to marketing them. It's the process of making the pop-ups that's the key to it all, which is again something that no one has ever written about. Even to this day no one does it, and I haven't told anybody, and I'm sorry, but I'm not telling you here either. Maybe I'll write it in my will so it's read at my will reading, and ask it to be announced after my death, but that's one little edge that I will be taking to the grave with me, or at least until I think it's... Well, I don't know; I'm trying to think of a reason why I would actually tell people, but it's just not fair to the fish. Imagine if everybody was using them, and if everybody were catching 20 times as much as they do now, the poor fish wouldn't have any mouths left, so no, I'm not telling anyone, and that's the end of that. It certainly accounted for much of my success right up until I fished Yateley though.

Yateley was a weird one; I've got to say. It was actually the Copse Lake

Arlesey mid-20, 1982.

Winter, fully scaled low-20.

Hole in the Dorsal, also caught along the reeds.

(Left) My range of 'Pursuit' rods from Leslies of Luton.
(Right) Dave Moore under the bush looking for my carp!

I fished first of all; I only did a couple of weekends up there and caught Crinkle Tail using the pop-ups, so they worked, but when I went up onto the North Lake after Basil, I never had a bite. In the early years I only fished up there a couple of weekends a year, so I thought, well, knowing the class of angler that has been down here, they've probably blown, and they're probably not going to be effective. So I started searching around for alternatives, and also at that time, I was being offered unlimited bait free of charge from anybody who wanted to give it to me. I had the magazine, and I was a consultant for Nash and Mainline in those early days, and you know, the thought of rolling bait really didn't appeal to me any more, even though I had to roll the pop-ups.

I gave it a fair shot up there; I probably fished maybe ten weekends up on the North Lake, and because I didn't catch on these baits, these Legends, I changed. If I'd carried on using them would I have caught? I'll never know. They were tiny, bright orange pop-ups, and thinking about the fish that have been caught out of there over the years, dark baits certainly seem to have caught the fish most times – a dark red or a brown fishmeal type bait. That's what Bazil and Heather and all of them have come out on; I don't remember seeing anybody catch anything on a bright yellow or bright red or orange pop-up. Maybe they would have worked but I lost my confidence in them. I thought I had finally met my match when I got to the North Lake... I'd seen the fish caught a few times, and it was always caught on fishmeals glugged up in fish oils. The Premier lot had been fishing it – Jock White etc. So I totally changed my ideas on bait for that particular venue and went on the fishmeal and Robin Red trail as well, and I caught the fish. I caught Bazil on a Robin Red fishmeal type bait, and had another fish out of there and lost one. I ended up catching all the Pad Lake fish on it and the majority of the Car Park Lake fish on it, but whether I'd have caught them quicker if I'd have stuck with the Legend, I don't know. I thought I'd made the right decision at the time, and you can't go back in time so you know, what's done is done.

Anyway, getting back up to that first session on E Lake – it was certainly the first lake where spot-on positioning of the hookbait was so important. We had a quick plumb around; it was a very silty bottom, but under the overhanging trees and bushes was yellow gravel, and this was obviously where the fish did most of their feeding, and where they were fed most of the time. Most people fished and fed their bait under the margins so you know, where else would they be? I think certainly the fish came out at night, and fish were caught from the middle of D Lake during the hours of darkness, but during the day, they were in the margins. It was fairly shallow and there were people walking up and down all day; it was like a holiday camp basically. I'm not sure what it's like now, but at the time it was a holiday venue and people were up and down all the time. The fish knew they were being hunted and tucked themselves right under the bushes, and it might take you six or a dozen casts before you got your lead right under there.

We were there for the weekend; we'd got down there probably Friday afternoon and set up and just chucked them out anywhere on the Friday night and cooked up a little dinner. Thinking back, I think we went to the pub that first night and left the rods on the lake. If you walk down by the side of G Lake there was a pub at the end... was it called The Bell? I can't really remember, but I think we had a few beers in there, and then Saturday morning came, and I don't think anything had been caught – maybe one fish had been lost on D Lake. I had a chat with Al Taylor, and he was making every effort to get underneath the bushes from his swim on D Lake, and we decided that's what we had to do – we'd got to get it under there.

So I cast one of these little orange baits, and first cast it went right under there. I mean the trajectory of the cast meant that the lead just carried on going, smack right under the overhang, and you know, it was perfectly positioned. We were clipping up tight at the time; we weren't sponging or anything like some of the others with this high density foam, but we had line clips on and little bobbins on needles. Saturday afternoon, in brilliant sunshine, it roared off and it was a 25lb-odd mirror, which was a good fish for the day, and I was certainly well pleased with it. There's a picture of it here. That was basically it for that weekend, and we packed up on the Sunday morning, went home, and vowed that we'd go back next year, which was a strange thing to do really. We never thought of going up there every weekend or anything – that was our holiday weekend that we'd taken. So that was the first trip to Waveney, and my one and only time that I fished on E Lake. It was back to Arlesey after that basically, and a little bit of Stanborough, and fishing locally.

Arlesey was a great learning curve really; it was a very deep, very weedy lake. A lot of the action came from margin fishing, and it had a lot of lily pads round the edges. The edges were still very deep; it was almost sheer, so you were fishing in around 10 or 12ft right in the edges, about 6 or 8ft from the bank. I would make up a lot of small 5mm or 6mm boilies, from the same base mix as I was making my pop-ups out of, but I would colour them dark red with some Robin Red and red dye so they were very dark, and then I would fish one of these tiny bright orange pop-ups over the top. It was a lethal combination, and as I say, it certainly caught a lot more fish than anybody else was catching over there.

There were no 30lb'ers in there then unfortunately; I think the biggest fish in there was about 27-28lb. Certainly the most beautiful fish in my eyes in there was a fish called The Sub, which was just under 28lb when I had him. He was jet black, long and thin – there's a picture here – a fantastic fish. I caught him off the end of a reed-covered peninsula that separated the main lake from a little bay. It was on the bottom, on the same bait again, with about 30 free offerings around it. I was fishing opposite Dave Thorpe actually, and I was really catching them. I was doing evenings after work and catching fish most times I went down there, and I could see it was getting to Dave. It was winding him up a little bit and he constantly popped round to my swim to see what I was doing. But you know, I'd come up with a lot of things, and although I'm naturally not a particularly secretive angler, they were fairly easy to keep secret.

No one could discover my method of producing the pop-ups just by looking at the bait. As I said, it's totally different to what anyone else was using, and the critical balancing of the bait was something I came up with at that time as well. The philosophy behind it is that you make it so that it only just sinks, so that when the carp comes along and sucks it, there's no resistance, and it flies into the mouth as quickly as it possibly can, so they've got no chance of ejecting it. What I used to do for my counterbalance weight was put a little bit of 1.5mm rubber tubing on the hooklink before tying the hook, and then push a little bit of lead solder wire into the tubing. It was no more than 5mm or 10mm long, and you could just snip away at the lead with a little pair of snips until you got that slow sinking effect.

When people came round as I was casting out, they would see the plastic tubing on the line. Quite a few of them asked me what it was, and I would say it was a scarer. Kevin Maddocks had actually drawn a similar thing in Carp Fever where he'd got a bit of silicon tubing on his hooklink with a cocktail stick pushed in it. The theory behind it was that the fish sucked in the bait, the hook and the thin line, and then suddenly felt this much thicker thing on the line, which spooked them and made them shoot off and push the hook into the side of the mouth. It may well have worked, I've no idea; it sounds a bit ridiculous to me, but anyway, he'd written about it in Carp Fever and people were quite happy to believe that that's what I was doing. I never ever let on until several years later, well, when I wrote the first book. I decided I may as well come clean in that and let people know what I had been doing. I mean people probably wouldn't have bought the book if there hadn't been some little edges in there for people to improve their catches.

By that time I'd certainly developed into a much more open carp angler.

Set up on C Lake in the corner.

The awesome D Lake.

Setting up on D Lake, at last!

Simon Day with a C Lake brace.

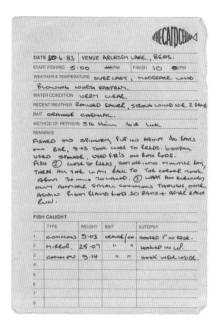

Carp Cellar log book pages describing the captures of The Sub and Hole in the Dorsal.

Geoff Kemp, bait supremo in the early eighties.

An incredible shot of one of the great history fish.

Henlow Grange produced a 44lb carp in 1983 (-ish), heavily spawned. I was straight after it, but it was never caught again and was thought to have died on its first ever capture.

I was born in the era of the secret carp anglers, those guys that I met first at Woburn and those BCSG guys that I had met pike fishing up on Loch Lomond were very secretive anglers. They were the matt black brigade, and everything was top secret, hush, hush and I was sworn to secrecy. They took me under their wing and when they told me things and told me that I wasn't allowed to tell anybody anything, so throughout the 70's, that's the way things were. But in the 80's, I went the opposite way and really helped as many people as I could to catch a fish. I was as pleased to see other people catch them as me; it reinforced what I was doing to see people being successful. I was pioneering things and it's very difficult being a pioneer and only having yourself to judge the catches on, but it's better if you tell people about what you are trying out and you get a few more people involved. I would come up with baits, flavours and rigs, and I'd end up telling half a dozen close friends who would go off and try them out. Some of them were instantly successful and that helped me to go down the right paths for the next thing. Some of them never caught anything, and it would have taken me a long time to realise that I was going the wrong way if it wasn't for the fact that six or ten or twenty of us had tried it. If it didn't work, it meant that I didn't have to keep on, you know, so it only a short lifespan and it was gone, and I was onto the next thing.

It doesn't happen these days, but honestly, when I was a draftsman, I would sit most of the day some days just drawing hooks and thinking about rigs and how I could develop things. I was being paid to design Vauxhall cars, but I was spending all my time trying to design rigs and baits. We came up with some fantastic ideas; in fact we came up with what is now at the forefront of carp fishing today, the chod rig. It's nothing new; it's just basically a hook with an extended shank. All the anti-eject properties of the top rigs of today were rigs that we thought

Carp Cellar log book page 1983 – the capture of the Leather from Waveney D Lake, swim 3.

of then basically; we've just refined them slightly in more recent years.

So as I say, I became a much more of an angler who wanted to see other people catch and to help them do that. I took lots of people fishing with me, many of whom had never even been carp fishing before, and I got them into it. Many are still into it to this day, and some of them are good anglers too. I'm not a secretive angler at all now, well, I'm not going to tell you about the pop-ups, but that's just one thing out of a thousand things that I have let people know about over the years, things that I have dreamt up.

So Arlesey was the place where I was concentrating on fishing in the margins, with a stealthy approach, and sitting back from the swim. Tight lines had become very much the vogue in the early 80's with line clips and everything, but I noticed from fishing in the margins that fish would bump into the line and spook. It didn't take me long to realise that a slack line approach was a lot better, and this was another thing that was totally different to what everybody else was doing. I went for a small indicator, pulling yards and yards of line off the reel, and letting it lie flat on the bottom way back as early as 1982 or 1983. I still do that to this day, and it has only become the norm over the last five years for people to put their indicators on the floor and have a slack line. Thankfully it was something that I was able to use 20 years before anybody else did it.

Several waters made the headlines around this time, and I got to hear of Savay, the North Harrow Waltonians and Harefield – all famous Colne Valley pits. But before I get onto the Colne Valley, which was my next port of call after leaving Arlesey behind me, I've got to tell you about the last couple of trips I had up to Waveney. The first one was with my good angling buddy of the time, Simon Day. We planned a week's holiday, and we were going to get on D Lake no matter what. We pulled into the car park, and it was absolutely rammed out. D Lake full, E Lake was full, and G Lake was full, so every swim was taken on our first three choices of lake. It was July and that was the time everybody took their holidays in those days.

So we had a word with the guys on D Lake and found out when they were leaving, and the guys in swims 2 and 3 were leaving on the Wednesday or Thursday of the week, which would enable us to have a couple of days in there before we had to go home. We decided to fish on C Lake, so we weren't far from D Lake, and if these guys decided to pack up early or anything, we could jump straight in there. C was a bit of an unknown quantity; I don't think there had been a 30 out of there, but there were some 20's, and there were a couple of swims which backed onto D Lake, so we dropped in there. It was an interesting couple of days on C Lake, and we ended up meeting a couple of people, one of whom at least I've remained great friends with over the years. It was actually after I'd moved onto D Lake and into swim 3 that somebody came and fished in swim 4, and that turned out to be Steve Alcott of all people.

But let's get back to setting up in swim 3 of C Lake... We knew that fishing the margin spots would be the thing, and close into these first two little swims were some bushes down to the left for me, and down to the right for Simon. We decided just to plop our baits out under these bushes and bait up quite heavily, and we had a nice few days in there. I think we ended up with about ten fish, something like that, and I've actually put a picture of Simon in there with a couple of doubles from C Lake. We had no unhooking mat of course, and the fish are on his lap. Mats didn't exist in those days, and it was some years later before they came out. In those days you just looked for a nice soft bit of grass, but you know, we still looked after the fish, and very few of them went back damaged in any way; in fact I can't remember ever putting a fish back damaged. It was very snaggy under the bush that I was fishing in, and a guy fishing further round offered to swim in one day see if he could free this fish that had got caught up in there, and that turned out to be Dave Moore. So yeah, way back then in the early 80's was my first meeting ever with Steve Alcott and Dave Moore. Anyway, after catching a few fish out of C Lake during those first few days, sure enough the guys in swims 2 and 3 on D Lake packed up.

The first year that I fished Waveney on E Lake, I had my 11ft 2¼lb test curve Sportex carp rods and struggled like hell to reach the Back, but on this trip, I had come well prepared. A new tackle shop called Leslie's had moved into Luton, which had started off in St Albans. They had a tiny shop underneath the flyover on Park Street, on the opposite side of the road to where they are now. I think it's a kebab shop or a taxi place or something now; I'm not sure, but that's where they first set up. As I was quite a well-known carp angler in the area, the father of the family, Leslie Crawley, a lovely old fella with two sons, Kevin and Ian, asked me if I would be interested in field testing some rods with a view to doing some Rob Maylin rods in their shop. Of course I was, and the first rods that I tried out were some 12ft 2½lb test curve rods, which later became known as the Intermediate Pursuit from the Pursuit range of rods. The long-range rod was called the Extreme Pursuit, the medium-range rod was called the Intermediate Pursuit, and the rod for fishing close in and anything up to around 80yds with accurate casting was called the Precise Pursuit, and Pursuit became my trade name.

You've probably noticed that Kevin Nash now uses the name Pursuit for his luggage and rods etc, and quite how that happened I'm not too sure. I

This place was spring fed and never froze in the winter. I only fished it once.

Dave Thorpe, a prolific catcher in his day.

Mid-20 linear from Arlesey.

Winter setup, 1983.

Arlesey 20, 1983.

was a consultant for Kevin Nash for about three years in the early 90's when I was fishing Harefield, and Kevin did ask me to come up with some designs for rucksacks and luggage as I was a draftsman. I could do quite intricate drawings and decided to use my Pursuit trademark for the rucksacks and everything, and I submitted the drawings. He didn't take up the design or anything though while I was still tied up with the company. I eventually left Kevin when Mainline first started up; I was a very good friend of Zenon's, and soon became friends with his business partner Steve too, and they asked me if I would use their bait. Well, rightly or wrongly, I don't know, I agreed. I mean at the time they were good friends so why not? I didn't owe Kevin anything; he and I certainly didn't fall out when I left Nash, and we're still great friends today. I'm writing this in April 2010, and I've just spent the weekend in Kevin's company, laughing and chatting about the old days, and he's going to write an article for Big Carp magazine entitled 'The Strokes We Pulled'. We were laughing about some of the things we got up to in the early days. But anyway, when I left, Kevin decided to keep the name. Some years later Leslie's decided not to carry on doing the rods, and Kevin brought out Pursuit rods and Pursuit this and that, and still has that name today, but originally it was my idea.

But anyway, back to moving into swim 3 on D Lake… I'd got my prototype Intermediate 12ft Pursuit, and soon found on my first cast that instead of struggling to reach the Back, which was only about 90yds away, I over shot by 30yds, and ended up over the barbed wire fence and 30yds into the field behind. So that was the difference that those rods made compared to the 11ft 2¼ Sportex carbon rods that we first used when they came out. I purchased them from the Carp Cellar on my very first ever credit card, an Access card. I actually got the Access card so I could go down and buy these rods and Cardinal reels. I remember it well, and how pleased I was to have this fantastic new setup. After having a whole mishmash of reels and bank sticks, not one matching another, it was great to suddenly look the absolute bollocks on the bank.

Anyway, these guys who'd had a week in swim 3 were interested to see what we were doing, and I was showing them the rods, telling them, "These are the rods that I'm going to do for Leslie's of Luton; they're a fishing tackle shop and you know, I'm going to be marketing them." Anyway, second cast, it went right under the bushes on the Back, and soon I had both rods out there. I've actually got my little catch report from that first day that says I caught half a dozen or so carp – three or four of which I caught while the guys were still there, including the Leather, my first ever 30lb'er.

I also met another guy who's still a great friend of mine – top Norfolk angler, Peter Regan. I shouldn't really say that because he'll get all big headed now, but I met Peter on that session. Peter was actually banned from D Lake for catching too many fish if I remember. The owners, who were friends of Peter's, wouldn't let him go on there any more because he caught too many. This is a coincidence, but only yesterday I was chatting with Peter, who had purchased a leather-bound copy of Pete Springate's book. He's now a book collector, and in fact he actually bought the last remaining leather-bound Savay book too. I re-launched John Harry's Savay book from the 80's, with a new section, last year and did a leather bound version of it, and there was one left. Peter started collecting carp books some years ago, well, he's collected them for quite a few years, but more seriously in recent years. He asked me if I had any leathers left, and I had one of each of them, so just before he went to sea, because he's still at sea, he bought them. He was actually talking to me about that session and asked, "Do you remember catching the Leather out of swim 3 on D Lake?" I said, "Bloody hell, you won't believe this mate, but I'm actually writing a piece on that now, and I remember it as if it was yesterday."

Anyway, it was a fantastic session. I don't think Simon caught anything in swim 2, and if my memory serves me right, it was probably because he couldn't quite get it right under the Back there. I think he'd still got the 11ft 2¼ rods and they weren't quite man enough for the job. Well, that was the best test I could ever put those rods through, that's for sure, and they must have sold a few off the back of that, because we had a big audience behind us, watching us get bites. I think we had two days or something like that in those swims on D Lake and it was fantastic. They are great memories, and to catch that leather carp too. There's a lovely picture of it here, which has never been published before, next to the lily pads in the corner of the swim. To this day, it's still one of the most beautiful carp I have ever caught.

That wasn't the end of my Waveney affair though. I did have a trip down some weeks later, actually, with one of a pair of twin brothers called Karl Pashley. The twins were only youngsters; I can't remember how old they were, but they must have been around about ten or something like that. I'd told Karl all about Waveney, and I could see on his face how much he would love to go up there, so I had a word with his mum and dad to see whether they minded me taking him up there, and they didn't. I took him up there for a couple of days as a guest, and we both fished. Carl has gone on to become a great angler, and I believe he has fished over at Elstow with his brother for most of his life. I think they're still over there now, and must have caught the fish in there dozens of times each. But that was his first taste of getting away from the area, the first and last I think, because as I

Dave Thorpe returns a 20 to Arlesey's gin-clear water.

Every one a beautiful Leney carp.

That's what we slept on. No wonder I have a bad back these days.

say, most of his fishing life is now spent fishing very close to home. We got in swim 2 I think, and ended up doubling up in there. If my memory serves me right, we didn't have a lot; I think we had a couple of fish, and I think the biggest was just over 20lb. Now I do remember that I'd actually put a picture of it in one of my early books, saying it was the ugliest fish in Norfolk – it was a short, fat thing, and that was about it I think for that trip, and for me with Waveney.

The trouble is that the Colne Valley came along... There was an article in the Angling Times by a guy called Peter Broxup, who was telling people about Savay Lake and the shoals of 30's that swam around in there. Peter was a bailiff at the time, and a new regime had just come in down at Savay, which had previously been in the hands of Ruislip Angling Club. We'd all read about Savay, or about the lake anyway, without it being named. Mike Wilson had been on the front of the very first Carp Society magazine around about this time. The Carp Society was started, I believe, in 1981, and the first meeting was in Dunstable. It was in direct competition to the CAA, and it was started by a group of anglers who had strong viewpoints on certain things, and were very political about the way they fished and wrote about fishing. The CAA and the BCSG were always non-political; Peter Mohan wouldn't have it, and he ran the pair of them, the CAA and the BCSG. Certain people raised questions about where the finance of the BCSC and the CAA were going, which was an awful shame at the time.

Whether Peter had a few quid out of it, I don't know, and I don't care really at the end of the day, and why shouldn't he anyway? He should have been on a salary. He was running two organisations almost on his own, which had thousands of carp anglers as members in regions up and down the country with regional organisers holding meetings for six months of the year, one a month, and it was tremendously well organised. The BCSG was, and still is, the upper echelon of carp fishing, and it's highly respected; it's like the royal family of carp fishing. Some people didn't like the way he ran it, and I'm not mentioning any names, but they were the ones who were turned down by the BCSG, and they got a bee in their bonnet over it. So they decided to start their own club and sod Peter Mohan, and it was awful what they did to him really. I mean the guy had done great, great things for carp fishing; he had brought carp fishing to the masses, and he lost a lot of publicity over it. Carp fishing can be very cruel to people sometimes.

Geoff Kemp was another. You see I bought my bait from Geoff for about ten years. He supplied fantastic bait, and then I remember something was written some years later about how the casein had been cut with another less expensive powder – I think it was whey powder or something. He more of less lost his business over it, and he might have lost his house over it or something – it was absolutely ridiculous. I mean I called him up and said, "Geoff, if you're cutting the bait, carry on cutting mine for Christ's sake, because I'm catching fish hand over fist, so don't go changing it!" He said to me, "Of course I'm not cutting it, Rob. Nothing's going on with it; it's just a lot of jealous people who want a slice of the pie. They've got interests in bait companies, or they want to start their own bait companies. They can see that I've got it monopolised at the moment, so they're sticking the knife in."

Sometime people can be so hurtful, and I'm sure they don't really think. Well, maybe they do think, but they just don't care, basically. I could fill the pages of this piece with things have been said about me in the past, and I hope I haven't been a horrible person to anybody. I certainly have tried all my life to be nice to people, to help people, and that's how I want to be remembered – as the guy who had time for anybody. Anybody who gets the slightest bit of fame seems to put themselves up on top of a box ready to be knocked off, and of course that's what happened with Peter and with Geoff Kemp, bless him. I bumped into him in 2009 down at Yateley Angling. I hadn't seen him for 25 years probably, and he's lost most of his hair. He used to have this thick yellow blonde bob, and I've actually stuck a picture of him in here so you can see. He was a very good angler, Geoff, and he knew his baits. Apparently he's into koi carp now and one of the country's leading authorities on them, so good for him. He's a nice fella and deserves it, and all those things should never have been said.

Anyway, I digress again… On the front of the first Carp Society magazine was this long fish, very leathery, with Mike Wilson in a very different pose in the way that he's holding it. In next piece, I'll have a picture of me in the same pose, the Mike Wilson pose as it's known. We actually put one hand under the chin, and the other arm across the body of the fish and underneath, so you actually had an arm either side of the fish. It's a very secure way of holding the fish, but most people don't like it because you've got your arm going across the front of the fish, three quarters of the way down the body, but that's what's known as 'the Mike Wilson'.

Mike had written an article called 'The Baiting Pyramid' where he was baiting a big lake. He was baiting up the entrance to a little bay with maize, and he noticed that the more bait he put in, and the more often he put the bait in, that slowly the big fish pushed the smaller fish out. He likened it to a waterhole where the antelopes and the smaller animals are drinking, making use of the natural resource that's there, but suddenly the elephants turn up and their sheer size pushes these smaller animals out of the way.

That's what he noticed with the carp in his swim, why it's now known as Wilson's Island – Wilson's Swim on Savay, at the entrance to the North Bay. This is the same North Bay, which became Tiger Bay with Maylin's Pads in it some years later. How bizarre all this is, this jigsaw of carp fishing that we put together over the years. I would never have dreamt, after purchasing issue 1 of the Carp Society magazine, Carp Fisher, and seeing that fish, that I too one day would be on the front of the same magazine with a Savay carp, and actually have a swim named after me in that same bay as Mike Wilson did. But that, as they say, is another story.

Rare action indeed in January. During the winter, on this very deep lake, bites were few and far between.

Chapter 2
Loonies and Toads — Pride of the Valley

*"Get him out, get him on the other rota, my
heart sank, I thought Roger liked me!"*

After catching The Leather from D Lake at Waveney, I couldn't wait to get back to Arlesey and tell my fishing friends where I'd spent the last couple of days, in particular a good friend of mine, Dave Thorpe, even though I knew that my catching that 30lb'er would absolutely do his head in. Dave was a very competitive angler, if not a bit jealous sometimes, and I loved to wind him up whenever I could. He'd been fishing hard for the old girl, as it was known in Arlesey, but unfortunately, and unbeknown to either of us, the fish had actually died and neither of us were ever going to catch it.

I remember walking down to Arlesey a couple of days after returning from Waveney and Dave was fishing down on the first bank that you came to, half way along, just before the Spinney. He turned round and said, "How did you get on at Waveney?" I said, "I had it," and he went, "No." I said, "Yep, the big leather." "How big?" "31lb 12oz," I said. I could see his face just turn green with envy, and I chuckled to myself. I am a little bit wicked sometimes, I've got to admit.

Speaking of being wicked, I've decided in this series to perhaps tell a few more truths of what happened in my fishing life. Some of the things unfortunately will always have to remain a secret, although good friends of mine like Steve Alcott and Martin Locke who spent those years with me said that one day I should write a book and tell exactly what we got up to, but I'm not sure the carp world is actually ready for that yet... maybe one day. But anyway, I'm going to be as truthful as I can, and hopefully not upset anybody along the way.

There was quite a lot going on in my life at this time; it was 1983 and I was planning to get married. I'd just caught my first 30lb carp and believe it or not, a 30lb carp in the early 80's was a very big fish. A fish of 35lb however was regarded as the milestone, and only the real top boys it seemed had caught fish over 35lb, and that was a target that I dearly wanted to achieve.

I decided to carry on fishing at Arlesey in my short sessions after work during the week. There was no night fishing on Arlesey, and I used to work from 9-4.30pm as a draughtsman, and then quickly get over there by 5.30pm and fish until 9.30pm-10.00pm, and then go and have a pint. That suited me, and it suited my prospective wife, but really I'd got big plans in my head of places I wanted to fish, and the prospect of catching a 35lb'er was really on my mind.

There were a couple of other local waters that we were dabbling on too, including Stanborough Lake in Welwyn Garden City, a day ticket water with a one-rod limit, which was absolutely stuffed full of carp, hundreds and hundreds of singles and doubles, and at the time I was fishing it, probably a dozen or so 20lb'ers, still regarded as good fish of course in the 80's. The other one, which we came across by accident really, was Fairlands Valley Lake over at Stevenage, another man made park lake much like Stanborough, with a butyl rubber bottom. We had no idea which fish were in Fairlands Valley at this time; we'd just heard about it from a couple of guys down at Welwyn Garden City and decided to go over there.

I was absolutely brimming with confidence around this time; I had totally mastered the bait. As I mentioned in the previous piece, I'd come up with a method of making pop-ups, which even to this day I've never seen anybody do, and I had amazing results from them. This was in the actual manufacture of the pop-ups, but something else that I came up with of course was critical balancing of buoyant baits, a term widely used these days, but a term that I came up with when writing a chapter about it in my first book, Tiger Bay. I remember sitting there in the kitchen deciding how best to express the weighting of these buoyant baits. It was the application of the weight that made such a difference to the presentation. There were a lot of people using pop-ups at this time – it was nothing unusual – in fact pop-ups in one form or another had been around for donkey's years, because people used to use balanced crust suspended just a few inches off the bottom with a little bit of pastry mix wrapped around the hook to sink the crust, way back in the 1960s.

It was an ideal method of fishing over the top of weed and silt, and a lot of people were doing it, but what everybody, without exception was doing was just squeezing a large split shot on the line a couple of inches above the hook. Of course this would sink the pop-up to the bottom and keep it anchored down firmly. What I was doing at the time was using a small piece of valve rubber on the hooklink with a tiny piece of lead solder wire pushed into the valve rubber. To add additional weight, I found a putty called Evode Anglers Weight manufactured by a Danish company I believe, and designed predominantly for match fishing. It came in a flat pack a couple of millimetres thick and about 3in by 2in square with a bit of removable plastic paper either side of it. It's much the same as the angler's putty that we use today, marketed under Heavy Metal etc, but nobody was using this apart from me. Nobody was critically balancing the baits so that they sank down so slowly that they just lay on the bottom as if an angel had placed them there with delicate hands.

Of course the fish, which were nowhere near as clued up as they are today, would simply come in and start sucking up the free offerings with a regulated amount of suck, and when pointing their suck towards my critically balanced bait, the bait would fly into the mouth and be down the back of the throat before it had a chance to inspect it. This proved deadly, and it still proves deadly today some 30 years later, so that just goes to prove what a devastating method it was, but to have it way back at the end of the 70's when I first developed the method was streets ahead of what other people were doing with their pop-up baits.

I had also acquired the latest carp equipment for the day, the 2¼lb Sportex carbon carp rods, the first carbon carp rods on the market, and the Abu Cardinals. This stuff was regarded as very ultra-cult indeed. So armed with this and my thirst for catching big carp, I was eagerly looking round for waters which contained other 30lb fish that I might pursue.

As luck would have it, I was working at Vauxhall motors with Len Gurd, who became a great friend of mine. We did videos together, and he did many cartoons and drawings for my books and magazines over the years. We socialised on holiday down at Zyg Gregorek's Anglers Paradise in Devon. I don't see much of Len these days, but hopefully he's reading this and he'll know how fondly I regard him. Len was running the BCSG in my area at the time, and had asked me if I would run the Carp Anglers Association, also in our area, and which was affiliated to the BCSG. So I did that, and I was going off to meetings with him, not only in our area but in other fairly local areas, like Duncan Kaye's for instance, in Northants, or Kevin Maddocks' and John Baker's up in Enfield in London. So I had met some of the top carp anglers of the day, which these guys were regarded as, and had become quite good friends with Duncan through writing to him about bait and big carp, and also from going along to his meetings. Len had a word with Duncan and asked him if he would mind me having one or two sessions on his Mid-Northants carp fishery up in Rushton in Northants.

The first year, which I believe must have been around about 1981 or 1982, I had just one day session with Len up on the water. It was a small gravel pit, if my memory serves me correctly, of no more than 3-4 acres. It was gin clear, very weedy and very rich, and at the time it contained one 30lb carp called the Big Mirror, a fish that had graced the pages of Kevin Maddocks' Carp Fever. For those of you who have a copy, it's the one that has the caption, "A 30lb'er caught on a single peanut." I remember how that caption affected me when I first read it, and I wondered how it was possible that this huge fish had been caught on just a single peanut. But of course, as time went by, peanuts, tiger nuts and everything else became a lot more widely used. Kevin was a great innovator of his age; he was the carp angler of his day, and preceded me by several years in catching numerous big carp from all over the country.

I remember turning up on this first session with Len and he pointed out a swim on a gravel beach and said, "Look, why don't you go in that one

The 'D' Lake Leather.

Fairland's 1983.

Thorpey with Duncan's Big Mirror at 37lb 12oz.

Fairland's common.

The Big Mirror from Duncan's.

there? It's called Kevin Maddocks' swim," and I thought, wow, I'm actually going to fish a swim named after Kevin Maddocks. Len quite cleverly dropped in on a swim on a large peninsula of land that poked out into the lake, a swim known as The Point, for obvious reasons. On this very hot day, Len began to feed dog biscuits. They weren't mixers; they were the ones that were shaped like a little fish I believe, and they were a salmon flavour or something. They were cat biscuits actually, not dog biscuits. I saw Len catapulting these out and getting one or two fish to come up, but I persevered on the bottom. I found it very weedy, and I remember finally giving up trying to find a clear spot, tossing them out in the weed for a couple of hours, and then giving up.

On that day, Len caught a fish off the surface on his cat biscuits; I believe it was 21lb, and I was gobsmacked to find that this was in fact Len's first ever 20lb carp. I'd had quite a few 20lb carp by then, and it amazed me to think that Len was running the BCSG, the most sought after and highly acclaimed carp organisation ever (and still is to this day), but in actual fact had never even caught a 20lb'er. That's no disrespect to Len; he hadn't really fished waters with a lot of 20lb'ers in. He used to do a lot of his fishing around the Luton and Bedford area, and had caught a huge number of double figure carp, but most of the lakes he fished probably didn't even have 20lb'ers in there. So, he was over the moon to have caught this 21lb'er off the top, and I was pleased for him too.

I had a mooch around, looked in a few likely spots, and found a little area across to my right and further up the bank on a causeway between the main lake and a little ditch than ran behind it. I think the swim was actually called the Sunken Bush swim. I put some hemp with a few crushed boilies over the top where I could see a sunken snag. I crept back for a look later on and saw a fish, again a 20lb'er, and I can still see it in my mind's eye today. I was so pleased that I had got this fish feeding down there. It was a deep, high-backed, dark, black fish, probably about 21-22lb, and it was feeding on the hemp. So I crept back, got the gear and moved into the swim, which was a mistake really. If I'd just brought a rod round I might actually have caught it, but I probably made so much noise and kerfuffle getting into the swim that it moved off, and of course I ended up not catching anything. I did nick a few of Len's cat biscuits, and actually ended up throwing them in the ditch behind me. I got quite a few fish taking, but it just didn't seem right. I'd gone there looking to catch this big mirror of 30lb, and even though I'd got a few doubles taking the floaters in the ditch behind me, I just couldn't bring myself to cast in there. It just seemed like somebody's garden pond, so I ended up not catching anything, and that was the first year's trip, if you like.

The next trip, Len called me and asked if I fancied doing an overnight session at Duncan's, and I said I did. He said, "Well, we can go down on the Tuesday and Wednesday," so I took the Tuesday off work while Len actually worked the Tuesday until four and then came down. I had a walk round but fancied that Point swim where I saw Len fishing the year before, so I called Len at work and asked him he wouldn't mind me going in there. He said that he wouldn't, and that he would be over shortly after work. Unfortunately he couldn't stay the night, but he said I was welcome to stay the night on my own, and quite possibly there would be other anglers down there. Well it turned out that Len arrived about six o'clock, just stayed for a couple of hours, fishing down to my right, and then made his way home. No one else turned up, and I had the whole lake to myself. I was very confident in the bait I was using; it really did seem to be something special, and everywhere I took it I caught. I had a little feel around, and found three little clear spots just off The Point. It had been heavily fished on there; a lot of bait had gone in, and I think the fish had just cleared some areas off. I dropped out about 30-40 of my special boilies around with my super-duper pop-ups, and decided to sleep out under the stars just on the bedchair. It was a beautiful July evening, not that long after I had caught the 30lb'er from Waveney, probably only a couple of weeks actually.

As soon as it got dark, the lake absolutely came alive, in particular the swim that I was fishing, with fish head and shouldering and rolling over all three of my baited spots, and I actually had takes on all three rods. The first rod went just after midnight, and weeded me up heavily. After a lot of toing and froing in and out of the weed, lo and behold, into a net went the Big Mirror. I recognised it from the tail, as it had a deformity that's quite evident in the picture with Kevin Maddocks holding it in Carp Fever. I popped it on the scales and it was around 31lb, still the biggest fish in the lake. There was another fish that overtook it some years later called Two Tone, which actually went up over 40lbs. I believe the maximum weight the Big Mirror ever reached was around about 37lb before it died, and Two Tone was about 28-29lb at the time.

Now I was in a bit of a predicament – I had nobody to photograph it. I did have self-take photographic equipment with me, but sacking was totally taboo. Duncan Kay had made a stand against sacking, and had declared in the newspapers and shows of the day how barbaric he felt that sacks were for retaining carp - he thought keepnets were far better. In fact Kevin "Sacker" Maddocks, as he was known, and Duncan "Keep Net" Kay had a fierce debate about it at one of the BCSG conferences in the early 80's. Of course, we know today that keepnets are far more dangerous to keep carp in, but Duncan was a very crazy character. He really liked a drink, and he had some crazy friends as well. I remember one chap, I think they called him Animal, as he looked a bit like that puppet in the Muppet Show that played the drums and would thrash around with long hair and a beard, who was his main drinking buddy. The two of them used to manufacture home made... well... they called them fireworks, but I think most sane people would have called them bombs. They would manufacture these bombs and play tricks on people, and I remember them actually taping one to the bottom of Peter Mohan's car. Peter was a school headmaster, very posh and very well to do, but he loved Duncan; the two of them got on well, and he put up with all of Duncan's tricks. I remember we were all out in the car park waving goodbye to Peter who'd been at the show, when suddenly this thing went off underneath his car with an incredible bang, and Peter went right off the road into a ditch. I think he thought he'd been blown up by the IRA or something, but of course Duncan Kay was rolling about on the floor laughing.

Another humorous story comes to mind... The carp anglers of the day, in those early days, took things very seriously. It was very secretive, and everyone was in matt black from head to toe so that they didn't reflect into the water. The start of the season was a bit like the Holy Grail really, and

(Left) A page from my Carp Cellar diary about the capture of the big mirror.
(Right) Diary about Biggins carp lake in Northants.

C.

BRITISH CARP STUDY GROUP

Fifth BCSG Carp Conference

at the London School of Economics
Houghton Street, London WC2.
on Saturday, 13th April 1985 at 11.30 a.m.

ADMIT _Rob Maylin_

Not Transferable

(Left) My great mate, Len Gurd.
(Above) Duncan was anti-sacking.

people would arrive several days beforehand to set up camp in their chosen swims. I've done this myself in the early days at Yateley and at Harefield; I've been there three or four days before the off. You'd be almost burnt out before you actually started fishing because you were on the beer and out every night, and by the time the actual start of the season came round, you were absolutely knackered and ready to go home, never mind start fishing. Duncan usually announced the start of the season in fine fashion, maybe with a rocket or something, or a little siren going off. Anyway, I mentioned the fact that Kevin Maddocks had a swim on this gravel beach, and behind him was a long, steep grassy hillside going up probably a couple of hundred yards to the road above. At midnight on the 15th, Duncan and his drinking partner were sitting at the top of the hill in Duncan's car, and everybody else was perched quietly in their swims.

You could hear a pin drop – their anticipation was building for the start of the season, and the chance to cast in at 12 o'clock. This was a fantastic experience that they were having on one of the premier carp fisheries in the country – these guys were the lucky ones, given the chance to fish this fantastic water. They were the top guys in the area, and very, very serious about it all. At a minute to 12, Duncan turned the headlights on full beam, and started the engine. Then he drove full speed down this grassy hill, straight into the lake by the side of where Kevin Maddocks was fishing with an almighty crash, and they ended up going about 20 yards out into the lake before the car actually sank. After a lot coughing and spluttering, Duncan and the Animal appeared a few minutes later crawling up the bank, pissing themselves laughing and announcing that the season was now officially open. Once again Duncan had surprised everybody with an amazing start

Anglers' Paradise holiday with Len and families.

REDLAND ANGLING SCHEME
1985/86 SEASON
SPECIAL 24hrs PERMIT

R.J. MAYLIN Esq.,
23, CONWAY DRIVE,
FLITWICK,
BEDS.
is authorised to fish at

SAVAY LAKE

ASST. GENERAL MANAGER
R.Pipkin

HOLDERS SIGNATURE:

Savay permit under Redland Angling.

Broxup, at the time a bailiff.

Ritchie with Sally.

*(Top) 29lb 15oz, my first Savay carp from the Reeds...
...followed quickly by this 21lb'er.*

Roger Smith tried to boot me out of the Loonies.

to the year, as only Duncan could.

Anyway, getting back to the point, he was totally against sacks, but I was totally against not taking a photograph of this 30lb'er. To this day, I have never told this story, but I sacked your 30lb carp, Duncan. I'm sorry about that, but yes, I sacked your big carp in my sack made by Del Romang. They were the only people making sacks I think at the time, and it's the guy who now makes Delkin buzzers, Del and I sacked the Big Mirror.

I didn't bother with the rod; I was far too excited, and just climbed into bed. I was only in there five minutes before the middle rod went off, and this also felt like a really good fish. It weeded me lots of times before it eventually shed the hook, so I didn't land that one. Before I could even get into bed, the other rod was off, the third and final rod. This turned out to be a really fat little pot-bellied fish of around 20lb, which looked very much like the fish that I had seen feeding the previous year in the sunken bush, but whether it was or not I don't know. I didn't sack this one; I just took a photograph of it on the ground and spent the rest of the time just looking over my shoulder hoping that no one came along. I was sitting there with no rods in the water, as it was pitch black, and I had no idea where the clear spots were. I didn't used to mark lines or anything in those days. I waited until it got light, which was pretty early, probably about 4am, and I set my tripod up and my little air plunger and rattled off about 20-30 pictures of the Big Mirror, catching one more carp before it was time to go, a double.

Then I packed up and went home, and actually went back to work I think that day. I was soon on the phone to Len Gurd who was in total disbelief; he really couldn't believe I'd caught this 30lb'er. Of course I told him and everybody else that I'd caught it at 4am that morning. Even in my book Tiger Bay, I can't remember for sure, but I'm pretty certain I said I'd caught it in the morning, whereas in actual fact I caught it just after midnight. The fish went back fine, and of course it lived for another ten years or more and achieved much larger weights. But that was a good little overnight session, and of course I couldn't wait to get back down to Arlesey and tell Thorpey, whose chin absolutely hit the floor. In fact he didn't speak to me for a couple of weeks after that. He actually joined Duncan's syndicate the following year, and caught a lot of fish. Dave was a very good angler and deserved everything he caught.

Around about this time I had quite a few lakes that I was looking at. I'd purchased a ticket for Biggin Lake in Northants and had a couple of sessions up there. I did catch some really nice scaly carp, and there was supposed to have been a 35lb'er in there, which is why we joined. It was advertised I believe in the Angling Times, but we never saw anything like that sort of size fish when we were fishing there, and we never saw another angler on there either. There was just me and another guy nicknamed 'Scoop'; one of the Arlesey boys, who joined, and we had a few sessions over there. It was a beautiful lake, full of lily pads, and it had little battered and worn wooden walkways going out into the lake, through reed beds that you used to fish up against. It had lovely, scaly carp and hundreds and hundreds of tiny little carp in there if I remember rightly, all about 2 to 3in long. They used to net it every year, and whether it had a 35lb'er in there, I don't know.

About this same sort of time, whilst still fishing Arlesey, Stanborough and Fairlands and the odd session on Biggins Lake, an article appeared in the Angling Times by a chap called Peter Broxup. He was a bailiff at the time on a lake called Savay at Denham in Buckinghamshire, a lake that only those really in the know had heard about before. In Peter's article, he blew the lid wide open, telling of stories of shoals of 30lb'ers that were relatively easy to catch, and the fact that many of the country's top carp anglers were on there in those first couple of years of the new syndicate. The controlling club was Redlands, and the guy who ran the membership was called Graham Rowles. Peter Broxup was a bailiff and the early syndicates contained anglers such as Rod Hutchinson, Kevin Maddocks, Andy Little, Lenny Middleton, John Baker, Roger Smith, and the syndicate head was a chap called Bob Davis.

Also working with me at this time at Vauxhall Motors' Luton plant was my good friend Simon Day, and it was he who pointed out the article on Savay Lake, and informed me that he intended to go down there on Saturday and fish with our other friend, Gary Bearman. He and Gary actually went down there on the Saturday, were greeted by Peter Broxup who kindly showed them around, and they fished on the canal bank. I didn't go on that first trip down there, which was just a day session. They bought a day ticket from the newspaper shop at the top of Moorhall Road for the grand sum of about £3 I think, or something like that, for a day ticket on Savay. When he came back to work on the Monday, he and I met up and he told me all about it, and we decided we'd probably go down the following weekend, which we did. I believe it was a Sunday, and we decided to get down there as early as we could. We stopped in at the newspaper shop, which was open early, and bought our day tickets and made our way down the canal bank. This was the first time I'd ever set foot on Savay. It had that same feeling about it that I'd felt earlier on that year at Waveney – this was the big league. This was somewhere where it was all happening, and it was a very exciting time for me, I can tell you.

I remember my immediate reactions to the place – that it was larger than I'd thought, and that the banks were very peaty with black soil; something I hadn't found before on lakes that I'd fished, I walked up between the canal and the lake, and there were several anglers fishing there. Because it was still on the border of dark and light, that first bit of dawn, they were all tucked up in their sleeping bags, but it was an eye-opener to look at the equipment, and to look at the bivvies. They had nearly all got what was called the Waterlot, which was a bivvy manufactured by the Carp Cellar in Watford in the basement of the Tackle Carrier, and it consisted of a Wavelock umbrella with the sides sewn in and waterproof seams. Stainless steel needles with monkey climbers were the norm, with line clips, and many of the guys there used two line clips down by the reel, one to set the hook on the take, and the second one just to make sure the hook was pulled in even further.

The first bivvy that we came to actually had little LEDs alight on the bobbins with some fine wires disappearing underneath a splash protection mat situated in between the front rod rest and the back buzzer bar. This was

Rod, top angler at Savay, my first year.

Lee and I film for London Weekend TV.

(Left) Albert Romp.   (Right) Seriously, Albert Romp and his pheromones...

…and master rig tier!

actually the setup of a guy known as Pete the Brain. He worked for the Ministry of Defence I believe, designing early computer software. He was very posh, and very clever, hence his nickname, and a bit of a wine connoisseur, as I remember. Later when I came to know him better and be involved in some of the evenings out to the pub and Indian restaurant, very often Pete the Brain would pick up the tab and would also buy the wine, as he was on mega bucks for the time. Pouilly-Fumé I remember was his favourite, and Roger Smith would always seat himself next to Pete the Brain, and in his squeaky little voice would say to him, "Are we having Pouilly-Fumé tonight? I hope we are." And of course we did, along with a whole

Jim Martinez aka 'Martini'.

bucketful of everything else really on most nights, but we'll get to that in a while.

We made our way down the canal bank past Wilson's Island, and Pete the Brain was a couple of swims up from that. The first open swim that we came to was the Reeds, and I decided to drop myself in there, while Simon carried on down the canal bank a little bit further to a swim called the Logs. We could see several other bivvies further down the bank from the Gravely down to the Birches, and these were actually owned by Jimmy Burns and his crew from Essex, who were early members of the syndicate, and again guys we became great friends with. It was so exciting to cast out that first time into Savay and to feel around with the lead for those gravel bars that became legendary. I used two rods only; one tossed out, as I later found out, to around the third bar at about 70-80yds, with a large lead for the day, which was probably only about 2oz, and the other was cast around the first bar at 30-40yds out with a 1oz lead.

Quite foolishly, I was only using 6lb Maxima hooklinks, which were nowhere near man enough for the job, as there were a lot of 30lb'ers in there. Around about 2pm the long rod on the legendary pop-ups of mine laced with shrimp and prawn oil was away. It was quite calm, with just a slight ripple, and as I had the take there was a massive flat spot out in the lake as a fish waved its awesome tail and careered off down the third bar, spinning my clutch round and eventually cutting through that 6lb Maxima hooklink like a hot knife through butter. I couldn't believe it was gone, and I can remember it to this day, although it was 30 years ago. The lead came skipping in with about 4in of hooklink hanging in the wind.

Jimmy Burns and his friends came down the bank to see what all the fuss was about, and they couldn't believe that I'd had a bite on my first day ever on Savay. I think at the time Jimmy was the only one who'd actually caught a fish that season; he'd had a 34lb'er if my memory serves me right. At the time, to catch a fish out of Savay was an incredible feat and people would do huge amounts of time on there, so much so that the syndicate had to be split into two separate rotas, which were affectionately known as the Toad Rota and the Looney Rota. In later years I was to join the Loonies, but for now I was a day ticket fisherman, something that the syndicate had to put up with. Very few people had actually caught fish out of there; Andy Little had apparently caught the largest amount of fish the previous season, and Rod Hutchinson was probably top rod the year that I was down there. Kevin Maddocks had caught one fish, as had Lenny Middleton, but John Baker was yet to catch. Albert Romp and Bob Baker had caught a couple of fish each, and they'd actually pioneered a section of the lake that hadn't really been fished much before – a large bed of pads off the road bank. The fish were obviously just held up in the pads there, and location wasn't a problem. They'd landed a couple of fish each, and Albert, being the character that he is, decided to have a bit of a wind-up with John Baker, because John was very interested to know what they were doing and what they were catching their fish on. John was very much of a bait guy, whereas Albert wasn't so much, but they decided to have a wind-up with John and it's quite an amusing story, so I'll take this opportunity to tell you about it.

On a week's session, the first week's session of them catching some fish down there, John appeared down on the road bank one morning and asked Albert if he'd had any luck. Albert informed him that yes he had had a 25lb'er. John then sat and told him his troubles and woes; how he had fished there a lot and couldn't get a bite, and was plugging him for a few clues. So when John went back to his swim on the canal bank, Albert and Bob cooked up a plan. They decided to tell John Baker that they were using pheromones, and as part of their plan they were going to tell him that butterflies were very attracted to pheromones. At the time both of them had the old-fashioned wicker baskets to carry their tackle in, as they were very popular. That day Bob and Albert set about catching as many butterflies as they could in their landing nets and putting them in their baskets. Not only did they put them in their baskets; they put them in their bivvys and in every little tackle bag they had – everything was full of butterflies, hundreds and hundreds of them. John Baker had said he would pop back later that evening for a cup of tea and a chat, and when he did, he asked, "Come on then Albert, what's the secret?" So Albert said, "Well you know, I really can't tell you; it's something that Bob and I have come up with and we want to use it a bit longer before we tell anyone about it." By now John was pleading, "Please tell us, Albert."

Anyway Albert got up off his basket, lifted the lid and woof, out flew about 50 butterflies. As part of the plan, Albert just said, "Christ! Bloody butterflies, they get everywhere – they're so attracted to this bait that we're using." John Baker's eyes opened as wide as wide, and Albert said, "Right, I'll put the kettle on." He opened the bivvy door and as he opened the bivvy door, woof, out came about 100 butterflies. "Bloody butterflies," he said again, "they're so attracted to this bait." John said, "Come on Albert, you've got to tell me, you've got to tell me." Many of you will know that of course John was a very good friend of Kevin Maddocks; they were big buddies at the time, and ran the CAA region together. John had actually just written Kevin's bait chapter in Carp Fever. Kevin and Lenny Middleton had the hair rig, no one else at that time had it, although John Baker knew about it, but he'd been sworn to secrecy. Anyway, John went back with his tail between his legs that night and said he'd pop down and see Albert again in the morning.

Come the morning, Bob and Albert had both caught another one each. The fish were just down in the pads; it was no secret, but they had been busy collecting loads more butterflies, and everywhere they went a cloud of butterflies followed them. In the end, John Baker, down on his knees, said, "Albert, if you tell me what you're using for bait, I will tell you all of Kevin Maddocks' secrets, all of his bait, and about a rig that he's using that's catching fish all over the place." They had annihilated Darenth on it, and another couple of waters, and now they were on Savay, and both of them had caught a fish on this rig, which nobody knew about, and which of course was the hair rig – the most devastating thing in the world. Albert had finally agreed, "Well, it's pheromones we're using, John; they're very attractive to the fish but also to butterflies and insects and that's why we've got so many butterflies down here." John was just absolutely amazed, and went on to tell them all about Kevin's baits, what was in them, what flavours he was using, and all about the hair rig, which ended up catching Albert and Bob loads of fish. Well, I don't even know to this day whether John Baker knew that he was being wound up or not, but that's what happened.

Back then the pub of the day was actually The Fisheries, which was a few miles away from Savay. In later years, of course, it was The Horse and Barge, the pub right next to Savay, which became the one that people used, but at the time it was the Fisheries. I remember going up there a couple of times before I started fishing seriously down in the valley, but at the start of the following year, I was up there on opening night…

I actually got into the syndicate the following year at Savay, joined the Looney Rota, and we were on for the first week. I chose to fish in Wilson's Island and tiger nuts were my chosen bait. I fished next to Jim Martinez who became quite a good friend of mine on there. Tiger nuts were something totally new, and there weren't a lot of people using them. Dicky Cauldwell had actually used them first the season before, but unbeknown to Dicky, Martin Locke and Dave Wibley had actually been baiting up the whole year with tigers, trying to get them on the feed. We felt at the time, or the theory of the day was, that tigers had to be introduced over a long period before the fish got on them. Well, we know that's not true now; you can catch them straight off on tigers, but they'd been putting them in over a period of time. Dicky Cauldwell had caught quite a few fish on them that year, and I went on at the start of the season using tigers in Wilsons Island, a swim that was famous because of his article in the Carp Society magazine

Top man!

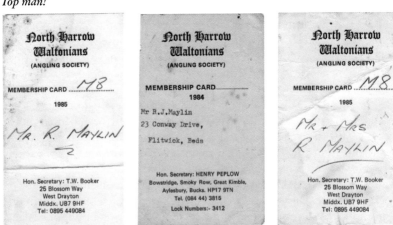

Harrow cards 84-86.

Rule Book

HON. Secretary:
Mr. T. W. Booker,
25 Blossom Way, West Drayton, Middlesex
Tel:0895 449084

Bailiff:
Mr. E. W. J. Smith,
Lyndhurst, Uxbridge Road, Mill End,
Rickmansworth Herts.
Tel: Rickmansworth 775798

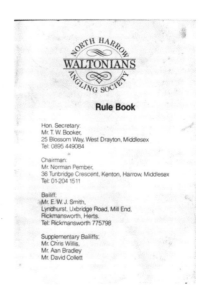

Rule Book

Hon. Secretary:
Mr. T. W. Booker,
25 Blossom Way, West Drayton, Middlesex
Tel: 0895 449084

Chairman:
Mr. Norman Pember,
36 Tunbridge Crescent, Kenton, Harrow, Middlesex
Tel: 01-204 1511

Bailiff:
Mr. E. W. J. Smith,
Lyndhurst, Uxbridge Road, Mill End,
Rickmansworth, Herts.
Tel: Rickmansworth 775798

Supplementary Bailiffs:
Mr. Chris Willis,
Mr. Aan Bradley
Mr. David Collett

Harrow rules 84-85.

Lee's opening day Harrow 40.

My opening day Savay 20.

Maylin, the 'Chinese Carp Ace', in all his
Bountyhunter splendour, inspects a tempting free offering.

MAY-LING – 'THE CHINESE CARP ACE'.

number 1 called 'The Baiting Pyramid'. Mike was actually using maize, but I went in there with tigers.

There was a large snag bush hanging over the water, and I ended up catching a fish of 21lb on opening day; a leather, which was quite unusual for the lake, as the fish in there were mainly mirrors. At the time, the commons in there were of course Sally and Sally's Mate, the big ones, and Sally had been out at 34lb that year. I had actually met a chap up at one of my CAA meetings who had caught it three times as his first fish of the year, and his name was Roger Smith. He used to come along to all my meetings, and I had some good chats with Roger about Savay before I actually fished there. Actually on the draw to see whether I went in the Loonies or the Toads, Roger actually pulled a bit of a snidey on me, and I heard him saying to Peter Broxup that he didn't want me on the Looney rota. "Get him on the other rota," he said, pointing over at me, and it hurt my feelings, I've got to say. I thought I got on well with Roger, but in hindsight I suppose it must have been that Roger didn't want the competition on his rota. I was doing nowhere near the sort of time that he was doing; he would fish full weeks on his rota, whereas I was only doing alternate weekends, fishing one weekend in two. But for whatever reason, Roger did try and put the knife into me at that meeting, but Peter had already made his mind up that I was going to be on the Loonies, and that was that. Peter ruled the show; he was the boss without a doubt and ruled the syndicate with an iron hand.

Anyway, getting back to the Fisheries on that opening day evening – there was a big celebration going on down the other end of the pub with some guys from Kent. One chap I had met once before, and I'd actually made a film with him for London Weekend TV with Ben Elton up at the Walthamstow reservoirs, on reservoir number 1. That guy was Lee Jackson, and he was one of the guys fortunate enough to catch a fish on that show; he and Kevin Maddocks caught one each. I don't think anybody else caught anything. Ben Elton, the comedian, was doing a show at the time called the Six O'clock Show, and he wanted to show the extreme lengths that carp anglers went to just to catch a fish.

Anyway it was Lee who was celebrating along with a few other of the Kent guys; Peter Ridley, Little Kevin, and Jimmy Burns, and they were actually fishing a water not far down the valley from Savay called the North Harrow Waltonians, a water that nobody really knew anything about. On that opening day, Lee had actually caught a 40lb'er – 40lb 4oz, I believe – and the whole valley was buzzing with the thought that there could be multiple 40lb'ers in this water. This was the first time that guys from outside of the area had actually got on there; it had previously been fished by local anglers who didn't have much of a clue in all fairness. Of course these lads from Kent went on there, and during that first season, Peter Ridley in particular did well. He ended up catching two or three high 20's; in fact a couple of 29lb'ers, I remember, and they actually named these two fish Peter's 29's. Of course everybody wanted to know a bit more about the North Harrow Waltonians and what it was all about. Well what it was all about was the fact that it was a no night fishing water where you were allowed on the water at, I think, 6am or something like that, and you had to be off by 8pm – it had fixed hours way back in the early 80's. It was actually me who campaigned to change the hours on there; I submitted a request to the membership secretary, I think the following year, or maybe even the year after, suggesting that they revise their hours to include dawn and dusk. I actually laid out a plan on paper where you were allowed on an hour before dawn and off an hour after dusk so that throughout the year, the times changed. It was more awkward because you always had to find out what time you were off, but it gave you longer during the summer, so you could get on around 4am and stay on there until around 10 or 11pm. In the winter, of course, you had fewer hours, but it really was a good idea of mine. The club took up the plan, and I believe it's still like that to this day, some 30 years later.

Anyway, Lee had caught this 40lb'er, and I decided to do what I could to try and find out how you obtained membership for the North Harrow Waltonians. This could be a water I could fish on the alternate weeks to my rota on Savay, still keeping me down the valley, and still keeping me out with the lads, as the social life was unbelievable. I remember that opening night as I was fishing next to Jim Martinez; he sort of took me under his wing a little bit, and he and I went up to the Fisheries and sat at this huge table with Rod and everybody else. By the end of the night we were all up on the table dancing and singing and out in the car park, getting up to all sorts of things. It was a fantastic social down there, and the Looney rota really ruled the roost of the valley. Anyway, we got to the pub and had a pint, and then ordered a huge meal of steak and chips and eggs and sausages, like a mixed grill, and all sat and ate it.

We drank and drank as much beer as we could and then about 11pm they announced that they were now going to the Indian for another meal. This seemed most peculiar to me; I couldn't imagine for the life of me why anyone would want to eat anything else, as we'd just had a huge mixed grill on a great big oval plate. But sure enough, up to the Indian we went, only to find out later that this was a ritual for the syndicate in that every night we all went for an Indian; it was the law, you went, and that was that. Believe it or not, this was the first Indian I'd ever eaten, and I found myself sitting next to Roger Smith, who informed me that he was having a chicken bhuna. I had no idea what a chicken bhuna was, but he told me it wasn't too hot and that I'd like it. He was having pilau rice and this that and the other, and a naan bread, so as Roger ordered his, I said to the waiter, who was affectionately known as Gunga Din, that I would have the same, and bloody nice it was too... My mouth's watering now as I'm talking about it... But yeah, it was a great night, a great experience. Anyway, I had the mother of all hangovers in the morning and didn't catch anything else from Wilsons Island on that first trip.

The following week I was organising one of my CAA social evenings down in Dunstable. I used to rent a hall down there and send out letters to about 300 members in the Bedfordshire, Hertfordshire, Buckinghamshire and Oxfordshire area. We had some good anglers coming along at the time, and some real nice guys as well, and I was very, very fortunate to meet Pete Frost. Pete was the chairman, I believe, of the BCSG, but always said to me that he never really was a carp angler. Bream were his favourite, but he got his position by a bit of a fluke really, and I'll tell you the story as he relayed it to me...

He was actually fishing Tiddenfoot Pits in Leighton Buzzard for bream in, oh, I can't remember the date exactly, but I'm pretty sure it was the early 60's. At the time you couldn't buy nylon line; it didn't exist, so what they used for line was something called catgut. I'm not too sure what the actual stuff was made out of; I've got a feeling someone told me it was something to do with the intestines of something or other, but anyway, it had its drawbacks. For one thing, it was very stiff until it was wet, so you had to pull all of your catgut off the reel and drop it in the lake for half an hour before it was actually supple enough to cast it out through the rod rings. But worse than that, it only came in 6ft lengths, so every 6ft you had a knot, and it was very thick. It was the stuff they used for stringing tennis rackets I believe, so you can imagine the thickness of it, and the size of the knot you had to have. Of course, even the rod rings of the day were nothing like what we've got today. The top rod rings, the Seymo rings, weren't around, so they were agate lined, which was an orange resin, almost like a clear orange plastic lining to the rings, and it made the hole quite small, so getting these knots through the rings was a job in itself. What they had to do was lay a plastic sheet on the floor and after they'd soaked the catgut, so Peter told me, they would lay the catgut in large rings on top of the plastic sheet, then put the bait on, which would be a lump of bread paste or something. Then they'd hurl it free-lined out into the lake, hoping that these large knots

SAVAY LAKE.........DENHAM. ....SYNDICATE 1984/85.

ROTA 1	ROTA 2
B. HANKINS	A. BARKER
P. HILL	B. BOLTON
D. WELCH	J. BURNS
R. HUTCHINSON	D. CAMPBELL
A. LEWIS	D. MOORE
J. MARTINEZ	S. CLEMENTS
R. MAYLIN	Z. BOJKO
K. O.CONNOR	R.M. WALKER
D. ORRISS	B. HEERY
C. RIGBY	J. KILLEN
P. SHORTER	M. KILLEN
D. WHIBLEY	B. MORRIS
S. J. HUNT	R. STALLARD
R. POINTER	J. LILLEY
A. ABBOTT	A. KELLOCK
B. BAKER	R. WALKER
J. BAKER	B. VARNEY
D. WOODS	C. HOWARD
A. ROMP	J. ALLEN
M. CUFF	M. LAWSON
M. WARREN	P. WRIGHT
B. JONES	P. REGAN
M. HATCHMAN	D. WHEELER
M. LOCKE	B. ASHBY
H.A. HOBBS	B. SPEED'
J. HEPPER	T. HALL
R. MCDONALD	C. WESTLAKE

ROTA CHANGES 4p.m. SUNDAYS............ROTA RUNS UNTIL SUNDAY 30th DECEMBER 1984.
COMBINATION LOCK NUMBER ON COMPOUND.......No. 5124
COMBINATION LOCK NUMBER ON CANAL BANK.....No. 5364
OPEN WEEKEND FOR REUNION FROM MIDDAY FRIDAY 23rd NOVEMBER UNTIL
MIDDAY SUNDAY 25th NOVEMBER.

Loonies and Toads 1984.

would find their way through the rings.

On this particular day in the summer down at Tiddenfoot Pits, blow me down if he didn't catch a 33lb mirror carp, a fish which I believe I'm right in saying was probably about the fifth or sixth largest carp ever caught in the UK, and it put old Pete right in the headlines. I believe he went on to catch one or two more carp out of there, but unfortunately the lake was actually hit by some sort of poison. The fish started turning up, but very quickly the specimen anglers of the day got down there, got as many carp out as they could, and put them in the canal, which ran nearby. I believe some of those original fish did actually live for a few years, but I suppose they're all dead now. There was several 30lb'ers in there; it was probably one of the most prolific big carp waters of the day and at the time, Peter Frost was fishing with guys like Peter Stone, Frank Guttfield, and Dick Walker, who was fishing in the area. These were the superstars of the day if you like, but Peter Frost was an absolute gentleman – such a nice fella. He lived in Luton, and worked at Vauxhall in the Dunstable plant along with Len Gurd. He would always come along to my meetings, as would Bob Baker, Richie MacDonald, Alan Downey, and quite a few of the top anglers of the day.

Now I happened to be chatting up at the bar with a few guys from the St Albans area who always came along to meetings, and one of them was a big guy called Len. I can't remember what his surname was, but he fished down at Stanborough with me, and always came along to the meetings. He had a red face, and he was always ever so loud, almost shouting whenever he spoke to you, but he was a lovely guy. I remember being down at Stanborough one day with him, and he always had to be an exhibitionist. We'd get on there first thing in the morning and he'd do press-ups, 20 or 30 in a row, shouting and screaming as he was doing them, saying, "Right, that's it, I'm ready to go now, fit as a fiddle." Unfortunately he died, probably in his late 40's or early 50's, bless him, but he was a lovely guy. Anyway, he was telling me that he was a member of the North Harrow Waltonians, and that in fact his wife Stella worked with the membership secretary, whose name I can't remember, at such and such a company. So obviously they weren't going to give too much information out about it because they didn't want people joining. Len and Lee and everybody else were keeping it under their hats, and trying to stop an avalanche of people getting into the club, but I had a little think about it and came up with a cunning plan.

I found out where this company was, got the number, and actually called this guy at work saying that I was a friend of Len and Stella's. I've never met Stella in my life, but with a little white lie maybe I could get myself in the club. "Oh," he said, "That's fantastic. Do you fish for carp?" I said, "No, no I don't fish for carp; bream are my favourite." "Oh well, send your £10 and I'll send you a membership card," and that was it, I was in – a £10 ticket into the North Harrow Waltonians – result.

Just sidetracking again quickly; I mentioned about fishing down at Stanborough with Len, and the story I told you about Duncan Kaye's opening night… well, I've got an even funnier one for the start of the season I did at Stanborough…

Stanborough had a car park on either bank, one on the riverside and one on the opposite side. On this particular 16th June, we were all parked in the riverside car park. It's a large car park; it was a public park and held upwards of 200 cars. There were probably about 30-40 carp anglers there waiting to be allowed on at the given time, which I believe was about 7am. Now for those of you who know the lake, you'll know that you have to cross a river to get onto the lake. It's the River Lee; it's probably only about 20-30ft across, but there was a little bridge, just a flat gravel bridge about 2m wide with no barrier on the sides of it, going across to the riverside bank of the lake.

Anyway, 40 anglers were standing on one side of the bridge when the guy in charge blew the whistle and said, "Right, all on." So 40 anglers, all laden with rucksacks, bedchairs, tackle bags, baskets and God knows what, suddenly crammed themselves onto this little bridge and tried to push their way across. Of course it was absolute mayhem, and about ten people actually fell off the sides of the bridge into the river, laden with all their tackle – rod holdalls, baskets and everything. Luckily it was only about 2ft deep, but what a laugh.

Chapter 3
Henry Peplow and the
Green-eyed Monsters

*"Unbeknown to me, the who's who of famous
carp anglers had also joined this year."*

Henry Peplow... Yeah, that was his name; it's come back to me now. He was the old fella who was running the North Harrow Waltonians at the time, and who I tricked into letting me join, saying that I was a friend of Len and Stella Simms. It was only a white lie, so please don't judge me too harshly...

Anyway, I was in, and it was a new water to the Colne Valley, which had only been fished for a year by any top class carp anglers. The previous year Lee Jackson and co. had got on the lake; Lee had caught a 40, and little Pete Ridley had caught a couple of 29's. I think there had been a few other fish caught but not many, but that was certainly about to change, unbeknown to me the Who's Who of famous carp anglers had actually joined that year including Rod Hutchinson, Kevin Maddocks, Ritchie McDonald, Zenon Bojko, Martin Locke, Dave Whibley, Bernie Stamp, Terry O'Brien, Keith O'Conner, Jim Martinez, Uncle Tom Cobley and all. No one knew what was in there after Lee's early capture of a 40lb'er. I think people were expecting the possibility of multiple 40lb'ers in one venue. Of course that wasn't the case, and Lee's was the biggest by miles. In fact Peter Ridley's couple of 29lb'ers were probably within the top six fish weight-wise in the lake that year. The following year, my first season, a lot of those upper-20's went over the 30lb barrier, but as far as I know, there were only a couple of fish that topped the 35lb benchmark.

Still working at Vauxhall Motors as a draftsman, I took a day's holiday on a Monday and made my way down to the North Harrow Waltonians. There were three car parks with two recommended by the club. One of these was at the end of the Barge Bay, a long, narrow strip of water with lots of lily pads in it that stretched down to the start of the islands. The islands then went down about half the lake, probably about 100yds long, I suppose, and then the water opened up into a large bowl shape area down to the bottom bank where the famous swims known as The Lawn and the Stump were situated. The second car park that was recommended was almost directly opposite the Barge Bay car park, at the start of the Islands on the opposite side. You could park in there if you wanted to fish in the left-hand Island swims down to the Canopy and as far as the Gate where the Islands stopped, and the lake opened out.

There was also another car park directly behind the Gate, but I don't think this car park was really recommended for parking in. It was a council car park, and this was very often the one used by the anglers who fished down the bottom end of the lake. It did cut your walk down dramatically, and it was also the car park that everyone used to sleep in their cars when they were doing more than one day on the lake. This first year, fishing times were around about 6am until about 8pm, something like that.

Anyway, I pulled into the Barge Bay car park, didn't quite know what to expect, never seen the water before and made my way down the Barge Bay to the Islands. Harrow was a particularly picturesque fishery, very well established with huge willow trees sweeping down over the lake, an absolutely beautiful lake I've got to say, probably one of the most beautiful gravel pits I have ever fished if not the most.

When I got down to the Islands, I noticed quite a few fish cruising around in the upper layers, probably using the bars. I didn't know this at the time but the lake was an absolute egg box full of bars, many of which came up to within inches of the surface. I dropped my tackle down in either the first or the second of the Island swims and decided to just have a little wander down to see what lay beyond the Islands. There was another car in the car park; I didn't recognise it but found a couple of guys fishing a little bit further down from me, and I think they'd lost a fish. One of them turned out to be a guy called Mick Hall. Now I'd met Mick very briefly once before up at one of Kevin Maddocks' and John Baker's CAA meetings in the Green Dragon pub in Enfield, Middlesex, and Mick and his friend Stuart had pioneered Lake Cassien in France. In fact I think they were probably some of the first English anglers ever to fish it, and on their first trip, they ended up catching a couple of 40lb'ers. They brought the photos along to one of Kevin's meetings and showed them to me, and I was absolutely gobsmacked. This was the start of the avalanche of carp anglers who visited lake Cassien.

Kevin Maddocks was soon down there after seeing Mick's photos, and his friend Paul Regent who had a coach company was soon running Regent's Carp Tours down to lake Cassien for a lot of the famous anglers of the day; Rod Hutchinson, Ritchie McDonald and John Allen to name but a few, and of course Steve Briggs who's still going down there now, bless him, some 20 years later. So I had a quick chat with Mick, and I got to be quite good friends with him over the next few years. He's a lovely guy, and I know he reads Big Carp regularly, so hopefully he'll be reading this and know how fondly I think of him.

Past the Islands the lake opened out and it all looked a little bit large and difficult compared to what I was used to. It was probably the biggest lake I'd fished up until this point, along with Savay of course the same season, so I decided the Islands were probably my best bet. It looked to be fairly easy fishing there – just a cast up against the bushes or onto the obvious gravel bars, which ran between the islands. So I set up stall in the second Island swim, pinged out 30-40 of my super duper boilies, chucked out the famous orange pop-ups, and ten minutes later I was away on the left hand rod cast to the left hand Island in the swim. It felt like an enormous fish, but unfortunately it went under the branches and I lost it.

Anyway, confidence was brimming, and I knew the bait would catch them. I recast both the rods; the left this time a little bit further away from the island to give me a chance of landing the fish, and I decided to position the right hand rod in-between the two islands in front of me on the gravel bar, bumping it up the bar so it sat on the top. I could see the fish using this bar like a little road to go backwards and forwards. I hadn't plumbed it, but I knew that it wasn't very deep because I could see the backs of the fish quite often in this area. There were just half a dozen pads that had been planted on the bar between the two islands, obviously by the controlling club who thought it would look pretty, and I dropped a little pop-up by the side of those.

It had been out there about an hour when the line began to twitch. I was fishing slack lines; I always fish slack lines, and I always have done. The line just started to pick up; I was on the rod in a flash and bending into the fish. It hadn't moved far from the pick-up point by the time I latched into it. It doggedly pulled me over the other side of the bar and plodded up to the right. Unfortunately the line was still caught around the pad stems, and I couldn't get direct contact to the fish. I piled on the pressure and pulled the big lump begrudgingly back to the pads, but still the line was caught around the stems and it wasn't looking good. I'd only got a 6lb Maxima hooklink on, and I was beginning to wonder whether it was going to be strong enough on this venue. A few minutes later, my worst fears were realised when the hooklink indeed parted, but not before I'd had quite a tussle with this fish up on the top of the bar. It disturbed a massive amount of water, and it was certainly a very big carp. That proved to be the end of the action for that day, but I was buzzing – absolutely firing on all cylinders.

Later that evening, about 7.30pm I was to make the acquaintance of an old chap named Jack who lived right next to the car park in the Barge Bay. Jack was employed by the Harrow Club to make sure that everybody was off the venue by the chosen time, which, if my memory serves me right, was 8pm. I suppose I must have pissed him off the following year when I actually got the times changed so that we could stay on a couple of hours later, which did mean that I probably interrupted his evening. I hadn't even thought about it until I did this tape, but the guy was religious about coming around at 7.30; he was manic about it, even possessed some might say. He would walk around the lake with his little Jack Russell dog and stand behind whoever was fishing, shuffling his feet, and saying, "It will be time to pack up soon, so make sure you're off by 8pm." He would do this to everybody, and he would be round no matter what the weather, rain or shine, summer

The Islands.

View down the lake.

Lawn end 'The 12 O'Clock'.

The Bench.

Mick Hall, the first Englishman at Cassien?

Springwood classic.

The Chiropractor.

or winter, bang on time. If you looked as though you had any intention of staying 30 seconds over the allocated time, he wouldn't leave your swim until you began to pack up, and then he'd been waiting down the bottom to make sure you were in your car and off the venue.

I can't imagine that they were paying him £50K a year to do this, but that's certainly what he was worth; he was like a guard dog on the lake and made sure that all the cars were out of the car park. Don't get me wrong; he was a really nice old guy and I had quite a laugh with him. I got to know him quite well over the next couple of years fishing down there, and he knew that I wanted to be down there until the last possible minute. It soon became evident when fishing the lake that you needed to stay there for that last half an hour. You could fish all day and have nothing, but certainly your best chance was in the last ten minutes before pack up time. The fish, through years of knowing they were safe once the light levels started to drop, had changed their feeding patterns to suit, and utilised that darkness to feed to great effect and to reach tremendous weights.

But back to my first meeting with him… He came shuffling along, saying, "Got your ticket, mate?" "Yeah, I've got my ticket here," I said. "Where are you from then?" he asked. I said, "Bedfordshire." "What are you doing down here then?" "Well, you know, I'm fishing for carp." "Hmmm, a lot of new faces down here this year… Things are changing, and I'm not a great one for change." He was a bit of a grumpy old sod really when I think about it, but as I say, we did have some sort of respectful friendship at the end of my time down there. In fact he helped me out a couple of times; one particular time when I had all four tyres slashed. This made it a bit of a problem to get out of the car park that night, but he came out at 10pm and helped me to sort out the mess I was in. Anyway, I'll get to the reasons for that soon, because believe me; I have never fished a lake with so much controversy, backbiting and jealousy lurking behind the scenes. As I told you, these pieces are going to be me telling the truth about what went on, and I think you're going to be a little bit shocked by what went on between me and the North Harrow Waltonians Club.

So rather than upset him on the first night, I began packing up half an hour early, and he was pleased to see me trotting up the path. However, I was buzzing; I couldn't wait to get back down, and on the way home in the car, I decided to call in sick in the morning and take the rest of the week off sick from work. Oops, been naughty again, haven't I? Well, I certainly didn't owe the company I was working for any favours, so the next day I was back there in the second swim down in the Islands. I'd made a couple of pounds of bait, and I put that in as soon as I got there, but there was no sign of

Micky Hall and his friend.

This was my first taste of fishing on the Waltonians, and it was somewhere that I was going to grow to love, respect and to cherish every minute I had down there. I don't intend to go through all the captures I had from this venue, of which there were many, as this has all been well documented in my books, Tiger Bay and Fox Pool, where there are chapters from the two seasons that I did down there. However, what I do want to talk about is some of the other things that I didn't mention in the books, and some of the extraordinary confrontations that I had on this venue. I never actually landed a fish during that first week on the water, but I think I ended up losing four or five carp down in the Islands, because I really wasn't geared up for the snags there. I certainly hadn't fished anywhere with fish of that size, nor with the gravel bars and all the other problems associated with the venue. My gear was nowhere near up to the job, but I did learn quite a lot about the venue in those first few sessions, and I was to pick up a few more tips from some of the other anglers who were fishing down there over the next few months.

Actually I decided after that first session to go back to Savay and continue my campaign there. I hadn't done any night fishing for some time, and having the bivvy up with all the things that go with it like cooking your dinner out in the fresh air and sleeping out was great. It reminded me of my previous night fishing enjoyment that I had fishing at the Vauxhall lakes at Woburn Sands and at Wyboston, but having fished day only waters since then, Arlesey Lake and Harrow Waltonians, I hadn't done any night fishing for a while. So I soon got back into the swing of things on Savay and was fishing my rota weekends every other weekend with my new group of friends, the Looney Rota, and the Famous Five of course.

I wasn't particularly successful at Savay during those first few months on the venue in the summer. I did land two or three fish, but it was a very difficult venue. However, there were things going on down there that opened my eyes. Firstly a very good particle angler from Kent called Dicky Caldwell was pioneering tiger nuts on the venue. Tiger nuts were also being prebaited by a couple of other guys who became good friends of mine – Martin Locke and Dave Whibley. So there were quite a few tiger nuts going in, and that first season I think Dicky Caldwell ended up with maybe ten fish, all on tiger nuts. I didn't fish them that first year; I persevered with the boilies and landed a couple of fish up to just under 30lbs, but that was all to change the following year when I went in on the tiger nuts.

By October I was getting the bug again for going back down to Harrow. Some of the other guys had been landing a few fish; Zenon Bojko had caught a couple of 26lb'ers if my memory serves me right, and there were a couple of other fish caught from down the wider end, The Lawn end of the lake. So I went down there at the beginning of October, and met a guy fishing down there. I can't remember for the life of me what his name was now, but I do remember that he was a chiropractor, and he'd been lucky enough to catch one fish out of there that season, a 32lb'er with a large moon shape scale up the top of its gill cover. He showed me some pictures of it and told me that he'd caught it down in The Bench swim, which was the next swim up from The Lawn. The Lawn actually became known as Maylin's Grotto, and was where I was to catch a lot of my fish. It was the last swim on the east bank before an out-of-bounds area, and it was one of the widest parts of the lake. It had a network of bars running parallel with the bank out in front of it, which I mapped out very carefully and measured my lines to. I knew exactly where all the bars were and where the gullies were, as the depth of water on the bars was very, very critical. I'd spoken to Lee Jackson who had caught several fish from the lake, and he told me that he'd caught his fish on billiard balls. I assumed from that, that he'd caught his fish on bumpy areas of the lakebed, but having plumbed them carefully, I found that a lot of it was far too shallow. If you were going to fish on the gravel, you had to be very careful where you positioned your bait so that you had enough depth of water. I would do this by fixing a marker float at a foot or 18in depth, cast it out, pull it up on top of the bars in certain areas, and then line these areas up with trees on the far side. There were lines of poplars opposite me, and it was easy to pinpoint different marks. Obviously if you set the float a foot deep and pulled it up on the bar and the float popped up, then it was going to be too shallow to put your hookbait on, but if the float didn't appear then you had enough water to support a fish tilting up and feeding. So I had these areas and depths and everything very carefully mapped out.

Following on from the tip given to me by Lee Jackson to fish on the bumpy lakebed, I began to catch fish down at that bottom end of the lake. The Lawn swim had actually got positions for three sets of rods; the left-hand position gave you access to the bank down to your left, the out-of-bounds bank, then there was one in the middle I think they called the Twelve O'clock, I can't remember for sure, and then one to the right. You could actually have three anglers fishing in that one swim, all with enough water to put a couple of rods out. On many occasions I did have more than one angler joining me in the swim – very often Ritchie McDonald, Jim Martinez, Keith O'Conner to name a few. Quite a few different anglers joined me in The Lawn area, but it didn't seem to matter which of the three spots I fished, I was the only angler ever to catch a fish out of that swim, regardless of who was in there fishing with me. In fact of all those anglers I mentioned in that list earlier, plus Kevin Maddocks, Rod Hutchinson, or even Lee for that matter, would admit that there were very few fish caught other than by me. I think the bait was the major factor; they absolutely loved it down there, and I was piling it in. I was rolling 5kg every night, which was a lot of bait for the time. It's not a lot of bait for these days I suppose, but I was putting it in every night in that Lawn area and they were on it, and they wanted it to the exclusion of everything else.

Anyway, on that first session down the bottom end, after speaking to the Chiropractor about the capture of the Moon Scale fish at 32lb from The Bench swim, I decided that I'd have a little go in The Bench swim myself. The Bench swim had a bench behind it, hence its name, and I didn't realise quite how critical this last half an hour was until this particular session. I arrived at lunchtime, put the float out, found some gravel bar areas with enough water over the top of them, and loaded them up with the boilies. I fished right through until the last knockings, and then of course Jack was

Drennan winner

THIS superb 31 lb 10 oz mirror carp was one of a quartet — including three over 30 lb — taken by Carp AA branch secretary Rob Maylin during just one week on a private water.

The four fish — 31 lb 10 oz, 32 lb 9 oz, 32 lb 4 oz and 29 lb 1 oz — were the first fish taken this year from the notoriously hard lake and fell to Rob, of Flitwick, Beds, as he fished a gravel bar with boilie special baits.

Drennan Cup winner 1984.

The enthusiastic bailiff, Jack, and dog.

My first carp from the Bench.

My diary entry for 'Moonscale'.

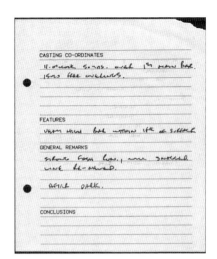

Next capture from the Lawn.

Rod was struggling.

Simon in action on the Lawn.

round with his Jack Russell standing behind me, shuffling around, going, "Time to pack up, time to pack up." I started to pack everything away – even the landing net – all except the rods, which I put down on the ground. Then, just out the corner of my ear, I heard a little click and the rustling of line coming off one of the two rods sitting on the floor. I put my hand down and sure enough, the line was coming off the spool on the left hand rod.

Instinctively I clicked the bail arm over, pulled into the fish, and immediately it was locked up behind the bar, as the line used to just go round the stones. I'd stepped up the gear by then and gone up to 15lb line straight through, which was much better towrope for pulling these big chunks over the bar. Half way through the fight I realised that the landing net wasn't set up, so I had to take the bale arm off, put the rod back down on the ground and set the landing net up. Well, sometimes your luck's in and sometimes it isn't, but it was this time, and the fish was still on. After a lot of toing and froing, using The Bench as a vantage point, I was standing on it and absolutely heaving the fish over the top of a 6ft vertical wall with only a foot of water on the top of it. It was spectacular to say the least, and into the net went my first carp from North Harrow Waltonians. Strangely enough, it was the same fish that the Chiropractor had shown me – I recognised the moon shaped scale on its shoulder. Again it weighed around about 32lb, but I can't remember the ounces. I actually put it in the Angling Times that week for the Drennan Cup and it won. It was a lovely fish, which went on to be one of the really big fish in the lake. So that was my first blood, and all that I needed to fire my enthusiasm back up to get back down there again and to fish those last couple of hours up to dark.

On my next session down, I went in The Lawn. I'd given my long time fishing companion Simon Day a call and told him of my success. I told him he should get his bum in gear and get down and join me. I'd actually got Simon in earlier in the year, which was my first confrontation, funnily enough, with a guy called Graham who was on the committee. I told Simon that I'd got a ticket for the Waltonians, and he asked me if it would be possible to have a walk around and have a look at it. So, rightly or wrongly, I took him down there, and we were actually up in the Barge Bay having a look when this chap came along and asked me for my ticket. Actually, because it was the closed season, the ticket hadn't actually been issued as yet, so I said, "Well, I haven't got my ticket because they're not coming out in the post until next week, I believe." He went off in a bit of a huff, and this was the start of many confrontations with this guy. He did set out to have quite a vendetta against me, as you will see as we go through the story.

Anyway, Simon had applied and joined, and he came down to join me on The Lawn a few days later. It was an afternoon and evening session, and I ended up catching a beautiful plate shaped mirror, again of 32lb, out of The Lawn swim. The following evening, on my own this time as Simon couldn't make it, I had a fish of 29lb too, and so it went on down there over the next few months. I was very successful on the venue; in fact out of my first six fish from Harrow, five of them were over 30lb, and the smallest of the six was that 29lb'er that I'd caught on my second session down on The Lawn. These were the fish that had been upper-20's the previous year; they'd all gone over the magical 30lb barrier that season. I soon picked up quite a lot of new friends, as you can imagine, as I was being so successful on The Lawn. With the onset of winter, quite a few of these guys were keen to fish with me and joined me on The Lawn in either one of the adjacent swims.

Around about this time, I also met another member of the club who was later to be on the committee, a guy by the name of Trevor Willoughby, and I was to have quite a few confrontations with this guy too, I can tell you. I remember one particular Saturday, I was sat down in The Lawn swim and in the afternoon along came Trevor for a little chat. "How are you doing, Rob?" You know, all the niceties… "You won't be fishing tomorrow then" he said to me, and I said, "Well, I had actually planned on coming down tomorrow," He said, "Oh no, there's a match down here tomorrow and the lake's closed." "Oh," I said. "Well obviously I won't be down then if there's a match on, Trevor." He said, "I thought you'd want to know that."

Anyway on the Sunday I was sitting at home thinking about this match, and the fact that it would probably be over in the afternoon, so it might be an opportunity for me to drop in behind the angler who'd been lucky enough to draw that peg, and then I could fish the Sunday evening in the swim. So after having my lunch on Sunday, I decided to have a drive down the lake, and who do you think was in The Lawn swim? None other than Trevor Willoughby. I said, "I thought you said there was a match on?" "Oh yeah, there is a match on," he said. "But they decided not to peg this swim in the end, so I thought I'd drop in for the day." Hmmm, yeah, a likely story, I thought. Anyway, if that's how he wanted to play it, then that's the way I would play it.

One of my next captures from this area was a 34lb part linear. I had seen this fish caught previously on the opposite bank to me by Jimmy Burns actually, and scooted round there to do some photographs for him. It was a beautiful fish, certainly one of the largest fish in the lake, and a fish which was to be made famous a few weeks later when it appeared on the front of the Angling Times at a supposed weight of 46lb caught by a chap called Dearman. I recognised the fish immediately as the 34lb'er that Jimmy Burns and I had caught some weeks earlier, and I knew that no way could it be 46lb. Ritchie McDonald was on the phone to me, and I remember him saying, "That's it, Harrow's done another 40, so there are definitely two in there." I said to him, "No, it's not a 40, Rich; it's a fish that I caught only a couple of weeks ago at 34lb." When we looked into it a bit deeper, it came to light that the angler had only got scales weighing up to 30lb, and had actually put two sets of scales back to back and incorrectly weighed the fish at 46lb. As this fish had no name, I decided that it was a good idea probably to call it Dearman's Fish from then on, and that's what it became known as.

Ritchie McDonald had become a close friend over this period, and he was desperate to get in on the action, as he hadn't caught anything all year from the Waltonians. He accompanied me in The Lawn swim almost every time I fished over the winter, and we did have a bit of a falling out. We're best of friends now, and I am sure he won't mind me telling the story because it is very, very funny, but before I do, I must tell you the story of how I first met Ritchie McDonald… It was in 1981 actually, a couple of years before this, and I was down on Savay fishing in the Log swim as a day ticket angler. I was totally unknown, and no one had ever heard of me, as I hadn't caught a lot of big fish up until then, but I was fishing Savay on day ticket and was in one of the best swims in the winter. Anyway, I was sitting back enjoying a little bit of winter sunshine on my face when along came this guy in a blue tartan hat and Barbour jacket, loaded up with gear. He trudged up the bank, huffing, puffing and wheezing, and stopped in my swim.

I turned round to him and said, "Alright mate. It's hard work getting all that tackle up here, innit?" "Oh dear," he said. "I've got such a hangover…" So I said, "Out on a session last night, then?" "Yeah," he said. "I was at one of these carp shows and had a skin full of beer." So I said, "Oh, I run the Carp Anglers Association in my area up in Luton in Bedfordshire. Where were you?" He said he was down in Feltham, and I said, "Was it a good night then?" He said, "Yeah, we had a great night." I said, "Who was the speaker?" He looked at me and said, "Well, I was…" So I looked back at him and I said, "Well who are you, then?" He looked at me, put his hands on his hips and he went, "Who am I? Who am I? Who the f***king hell am I? I'm Ritchie McDonald, that's who I am." Well you know, I was a bit gobsmacked, as he was one of the big heroes of the day and I hadn't recognised him, so I said, "Oh, I'm ever so sorry, Ritchie; I didn't know who you were, mate." I could see he was really put out that I hadn't recognised who he was, being a big superstar of the day.

Anyway over the next year or so I was to bump into him on odd occasions, and of course when I was fishing down at Harrow and having it right off, he was my number one friend, and we sat side-by-side. Sometimes I was on the right and he was on the left, or sometimes the other way round with Jim Martinez in the middle, and Keith O'Conner sometimes joined us as well. But every single time we were there, there'd be a bite and it would be on my rods. I don't think Ritchie had ever had this sort of thing before. I mean he was the man; he was the one who had the bites normally, and he wasn't used to some little whippersnapper catching all the fish, and it got to him in the end. It would have got to anybody to be fair, but the old green-eyed monster suddenly appeared in him.

It all came to a head one day when I had a bite at around lunchtime on a beautiful December day. I saw Ritchie get up and get the landing net, and he had a little tut as I was playing it in. It was putting up quite a scrap, and after a couple of minutes he said, "Come on then, get it in," and I said, "It feels like a good'un, Rich." With that he slung the net down on the floor, went and sat back down on his bedchair and said, "Well give us a shout when you're ready to net it then." So I carried on playing the fish and it came up and I could see a sort of network of veins running down the side of it. I'd never seen the fish before, but it looked as though it was a good'un. I said, "I think it's ready for the net, Rich," and he got up. All the time I was playing it, I could see a bloke watching me through binoculars from the other side of the lake, and gradually this chap had walked round the lake, round the out-of-bounds, and as Ritchie stuck the net under the fish, he was actually standing behind a tree about 40yds up the bank, still looking through his binoculars, which I thought was a bit out of order to be honest.

I was a pretty open angler and didn't have a lot of secrets or anything. I mean I've had blokes sitting on my shoulders, watching everything I did, so it wasn't as if I was secretive of anything. I just didn't like the way this chap was going about it. So after a bit more tutting and umming and ahhing, Ritchie took the pictures of the fish, which weighed 35lb 8oz, and was a fish that to my knowledge hadn't been caught. It was covered in veins and I called it The Veiny One, stuck it back, and this chap was still standing behind the tree. He hadn't come over for a look while we were doing the photographs; he was just sort of sneakily looking. Anyway, he came walking up the bank, looked at me, and he said, "Any luck, mate?" I knew that he'd seen what I'd caught because I'd seen him watching me all the time, so I said, "No mate, nothing." So he said, "Oh, alright then," and off he went. Ritchie turned round to me and said, "What did you say that for?" I said, "Well you saw him watching me on the other side with the binoculars, and he'd been standing under that tree looking at me. He knows I caught one,

Moonscale again.

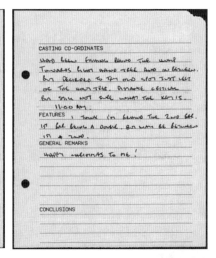

Christmas cracker.

First from the Lawn.

Lee's first 30.

The end of Ritchie.

Essex Jon, a mad mother…

Jimmy Burns with Dearman's.

so why come up to me and ask me if I caught anything?"

Ritchie absolutely flew off the handle at me, and said, "I don't like anglers who lie! You should have told him the truth!" I said, "Calm down, Ritchie. The bloke knew that I'd caught one. I just didn't like the way he was sneakily going about what he was doing." He said, "Well I can't be associated with people who are going to tell lies, so I'm not going to be able to fish with you any more." He packed all his gear up, slung his rucksack over his shoulder and started walking up the path away from me.

With that, my other rod that was still out suddenly shot off and the buzzer sounded. I was looking at Ritchie in disbelief; he froze on the spot and didn't look round. He was obviously thinking, bloody hell, he's got another one – shall I stop and do the pictures and weigh-in, or shall I go? He stood there for about 30 seconds without turning round, and then started walking off again. By then I was into the fish, which ended up being another good one, but somebody else had to come round and photograph it. So that was our little falling out if you like, Ritchie and I.

At that time Ritchie was close pals with Jim Martinez who had also been fishing with us, but since he couldn't fish with me at all now, he started fishing with Jim all the time. Jim actually told me quite a funny story, which happened some few weeks later. I continued catching fish down there, and due to the fact that I was getting them all off The Lawn, other people quite rightly started getting in the swim before me. I was forced out of that area and down on to the bottom bank, but I did some homework down there. I was befriended at the time by one of the bailiffs who I sort of took under my wing if you like, and his name was Alan Bradley. I think he died at an early age, and I've got a feeling he was related to Pete Broxup. There's just something in the back on my mind that somebody told me he was his nephew or something, and he died in his forties, which was bit of a shame. Anyway, I took this guy under my wing and he wanted to see how I was going about catching them. So we started fishing, he and I, down at the bottom end of the lake, which was much quieter, and lo and behold, of course I started catching down there.

On this particular day, Jim Martinez told me that that he and Ritchie were lying out on the bedchairs. They'd slept in the car overnight and were down first thing in the morning. It was very tiring fishing like this; most anglers would sleep in the car, and as soon as they could get down to the lake and get the rods out, they'd stretch out on the bedchair with a sleeping bag and get their heads down for an hour or two. So Ritchie and Jim were fishing opposite The Lawn, lying side-by-side on bedchairs, having a little nap when Jim was woken up by Ritchie having a dream. Apparently Ritchie was grunting and shaking and twitching, and this went on for a couple of minutes, as he was obviously having some sort of nightmare. Suddenly Ritchie sat bolt upright in bed and looked at Jim with his eyes wide with disbelief. Jim said, "What is it, Ritchie?" He answered, "Maylin ain't had one, has he?" Jim said, "No," and Ritchie said, "Oh, thank f**k for that," and sat back down on the bed. So I'd obviously gotten to the poor old sod to the stage where he was having nightmares about me catching them.

Probably about 12 months later at one of the shows, I was doing a talk and Ritchie came up to me after the talk and said, "Rob, you know, I was a bit out of order there, mate. I'm sorry about that and I hope you understand and that we can be friends from now on," and shook my hand. Fair play to him, and we went on from that point to have a really good relationship. I fished with Ritchie down at Yateley after that, and he was a very successful angler down there. I struggled, but after catching Bazil he rattled out the Pad Lake 40, Jumbo and Heather all within a couple of days of each other. So, what goes around comes around, and he had his share as well.

Actually I've got another funny story that I must tell you about Ritchie, which is hilarious. I was fishing at Harefield some years later with Essex Jon. Essex Jon was a big bodybuilder from Essex, and all the girls really loved him. He was such a big lairy, mouthy character, but great fun to fish with. We were both fishing on Harefield, and he was fishing down on this little hump of land that I filmed Harefield Haulin' on some years later. It was August Bank Holiday Monday and I'd woken up with a thumping headache up on the Causeway Bank. It was a beautiful sunny day, flat calm, and I thought to myself, what the bloody hell are we doing here? The beaches would be packed with gorgeous women with their boobs out, so what the hell are we doing fishing Harefield? We should get ourselves down to Brighton or somewhere and have a day on the beach.

So I wound the rods in and wandered up to where Essex was fishing out on one of the little Island humps, and I was greeted by the weirdest sight. He was lying naked on the floor, and when he stood up, he had an enormous erection, and I said, "What the hell are you doing?" He said, "I'm lying in that ants' nest." He was a bit of a masochist, and he was laying naked, face down in a bloody red ants' nest, letting them bite him all over. It was obviously having the desired effect by the look of him. He roared with laughter like only Essex could, and we both fell about laughing. What an absolute nutcase!

So he said, "What's up, then?" I said, "What are we doing here? It's a beautiful sunny bank holiday, we ought to be down at the seaside." "Right," he said. "Come on, let's go down to Brighton." He had a big red pickup truck at the time and we jumped in it, and off down the road we went. Anyway, as we were heading off I said, "Where's Ritchie?" Jon said, "Oh, he's on the…" I can't remember if it was the Fisheries or the Cons now, but he was on one of the waters down there. So I said, "Come on, let's go down and get him. Let's kidnap him and take him down to the coast." He said, "How are we going to get him?" I said, "We'll just tell him we're going to the pub."

So we pulled up alongside the lake and shouted over the fence, "Ritchie, Ritchie, where are you?" Ritchie said, "Shush, shush, be quiet; they're hot over here and they don't like any noise or anything. You've got to be really quiet and respectful. What's happening?" I said, "We're going down the pub for an hour," and he said, "Look, I've got a 60-minute rule on here; I'm not allowed to be off the rods for more than that, so if you take me up the pub, you've got to bring me back." "Yeah, yeah, come on then, jump in…" So he jumped in the middle on the front seat of this pickup truck , and there was Essex on one side, all 18 stone of him, and me the other side, not much under 18 stone, and little Ritchie in the middle. We flew down the road and straight up the slip road onto the M25 with Ritchie shouting and hollering and wriggling in the middle, "Where are we going, you mad sods, where are we going?" We were laughing our heads off, and we said, "We're going to Brighton." "No, no, you can't take me to Brighton! I've got to get back to the lake, or I'll lose my ticket!" We said, "No way Ritchie, we've got you now." So down to Brighton we went with him moaning all the way that he'd be in trouble when he got back.

Anyway when we got down there he soon forgot about the lake, and we had a great time. Old Essex was strutting down the beach with all his muscles shining, and we went to the fair. We had fish and chips, jellied eels, about ten pints of beer, and we ended up on the waltzer. Big Essex John said, "I'm scared; I ain't going on it," and we absolutely fell about. "What do you mean, you're scared?" "I don't like those things that whizz you around; they make you sick." So we said, "Don't be such a wuss, whatever's the matter with you?" Ritchie was really giving it large because as a youngster he used to work at a fair on the waltzer. I don't know if you remember the waltzer; it's like a chair that spins round, but you go up and down as well, and you can spin them faster too, and it really does make your bloody head swim.

Anyway, we got on this thing, and we managed to get Essex on there as well. Of course Ritchie stood up straight away and was standing on the back of the chair, holding on to the pole, and the fairground bloke did his nut. "Oi, you! Get off of there and sit down!" Ritchie was going, "It's alright; I

Car repairs on The Lawn.

Me with Dearman's.

Thirty number three.

More car repairs on The Lawn.

Back goes Veiny.

Steve Allcott and Kerry on a guest.

A proper winter.

Christmas Eve chunk.

Len Gurd drawing of me and Veiny. *Off goes Ritchie!*

Winter 20.

know what I'm doing, mate. I've worked on fairs." The bloke said, "I don't care, sit down, get down on the seat." Anyway, Ritchie was having none of it, and he was standing up and spinning us round and round and round. In the end it wasn't Essex's head that went; it was mine. I just couldn't help it, and I absolutely filled the seat up with ten pints of larger, fish and chips and jellied eels. The bloke went absolutely mad, and we all ran off down the pier laughing our heads of.

Come dark, about 10pm, Ritchie said, "Come on, we've got to go home." Essex and I thought we'd have a bit of a wind-up and say we were going to book into a bed and breakfast and have a week down there. Of course, Ritchie said, "No, no, no! We've got to go back!" Anyway Essex said, "Well I'm not driving because I've had too much to drink." In the end Ritchie had to drive back, and he moaned nonstop all the way back from Brighton. We did it in record time, getting back to the Horse and Barge in time for last orders, and we ended up having a couple of late ones there before we went for an Indian. It was probably about 1am when we finally got him back to the lake – so much for the one-hour rule, and what a good time we had.

Anyway, where was I? It was getting towards the end of that first season on the Waltonians. I hadn't had any more run-ins with anybody at this time, but the old green-eyed monster was definitely rearing its ugly head, and the following year it was all going to kick off. It all started the following year when I went down for my first session, which would have been in July time, and I fished down the bottom end of the main part of the lake opposite The Lawn. It was quite busy, and I was next to one of the regular anglers called Graham too I believe. Even more new members had been joining the club, and there had been some changes in the hierarchy of the committee too. I think Tony Booker had become membership secretary, and Trevor Willoughby was now on the committee, the guy who did the sneaky move getting in The Lawn swim by telling me there was a match on. Also the other guy called Graham, who'd challenged me for my ticket the year before when walking round with Simon Day, had actually become the chairman of the club. Confusing, but try and stay with me.

Anyway, I didn't know any of this at the time. I went down on my first session, and Graham said, "One of the big ones had to be killed yesterday." I looked back in disbelief and said, "What do you mean, one of the big ones had to be killed?" "Yeah," he said, "Trevor had to kill a 36lb'er down here yesterday. It was covered in fungus." So I said, "A 36lb'er? To my knowledge the only fish of that size in the lake was the 40, the one that Lee Jackson caught." "No, no, it wasn't the 40; it was a fish of about 36lb" So I said, "Well, have you seen the 40? And did you see the fish that Trevor killed?

How did he kill it?" He said, "Yeah, yeah I saw it. Apparently it was swimming around up in the Barge Bay, sitting under the pads. It looked to be in a bit of distress, so Trevor scooped it out with his landing net, bashed it on the head with his brolly pole and buried it up in the Barge Bay." I said, "You're f**ing joking, aren't you?" He said, "No, no, he had to kill it." I said, "Of course he didn't have to kill it! If it dies that's different, but fish get these sorts of fungal things, especially early in the season." He said, "It's something to do with the bream." I said, "No it can't be anything to do with the bream," and he said, "They put some bream in here and it's got fungus from them." I said, "I know for a fact, because I've had a conversation with Pete Mohan on another venue about diseases, that any diseases that bream have can't be transferred to carp! It's probably argulus or some sort of fin rotting fungus that carp often get. It can be treated; you can get ointment to put on there. No way should he have killed it! Have you seen the 40 on the bank?" "No," he said, so I said, "Well, that sounds to me like he's killed the 40. Don't tell me he's killed the 40, for Christ sake. What distinguishing marks did it have?" He said, "Well it's very leathery," so I said, "Yeah, like the 40," and he said, "It had a big moon shape scale down by its anal fin…"

Anyway, I said, "Right, hold on a minute," and I got on the phone to the two people who I knew had caught the 40 – Lee Jackson and Zenon Bojko. I said "Look Lee, a fish has been killed down at the Waltonians. Can you have a look at your photos, and give me a call back? All I know is that it's leathery and it's got a scale down by its anal fin." I said the same to Zen too. Within minutes both of them had come back to me on the phone and said, "Yeah, it's got the scale down there; it's got to be the one." So I turned round to Graham, and I said, "You bloody idiots, you've only gone and killed the 40!" Anyway with that, I had a take, played the fish in, and it was covered in fungus as well. It was a fish that I'd caught before on the other side, and that I'd christened The Chunk, which was actually Lee Jackson's first ever 30. It was well covered in fungus and it had dropped down to 27lb from 34lb the year before. Graham said, "Kill it. You can't put it back." I said, "I'm not killing it. There's nothing wrong with it. Fungus is a natural thing that happens, and if it's going to die, it's going die of its own accord, it won't die by my hand." I weighed it at 27lb, and then I put it back. The following year, that fish was 38lb; it had totally recovered from the fungus, and it had stacked on the weight and became one of the biggest fish in the lake.

Anyway, over the next few weeks, it obviously got around that I was putting it about that Trevor Willoughby had killed the 40lb'er in Harrow. When packing up one evening up in the Barge Bay car park, who should come roaring into the car park in his Vauxhall Carlton but Trevor

Fun on The Lawn

28 in the snow.

Exiled to the bottom bank.

The dream.

The Big'un before it got banged on the head

Mouldy Chunk, but still alive!

Back to good health.

Willoughby? He leapt out and almost grabbed me, giving me a right earful asking who I was to say he'd killed the 40. I said to him, "Trevor, you've killed the 40 for definite, but I'm not going argue about it here. Time will tell, and that 40lb'er will never be caught again; it's buried wherever you put it after bashing it with your brolly pole." That was that, and sure enough, the 40 was never caught again, but obviously from that point on, Trevor Willoughby, who later became the membership secretary, was after my blood.

A few weeks later I was fishing the same area on the opposite side to The Lawn. I'd gone down there after fishing all weekend at Savay. At Savay you could fish three rods at certain times of the year, and I'd got three rods with me. Now I realised that they were going to be after me, so I made sure that I read the rulebook from top to bottom. One of the rules in there was that all rods had to be packed away that weren't being used, so there were no rods other than the two that you were fishing set up on the bank. Obviously people had been using snide rods down there, and they'd got to hear about it, so they brought a rule in that any other rods had to be packed away. Tony Booker was the membership secretary at the time, so I phoned him up and said, "Look Tone, I'm looking at this rule, and it's a little bit ambiguous. It's saying that rods have got to be packed away, but all I do is I fold my rods in half and put an elastic band at the top and the bottom. That's how I have my rods whenever I'm fishing." "Oh don't worry, Rob," he said. "That's packed away well enough as far as I'm concerned."

Anyway this particular day in the afternoon, I noticed a couple of the committee walking round the other side, and as I was looking out across the lake, I saw a fish top down to my left, so I quickly wound in one of my rods and cast it on top of the rolling fish. The two guys sped up around the out-of-bounds, and came up past the Stump to where I was fishing. One of the guys, I don't know what his name was, but he had a shock of white hair, marched into the middle of my swim, past where I was sitting and stood in the margins, looking up and down the bank. He obviously thought I was using a snide rod or that I'd cast out a third rod. "Where is it?" he said. "Where's what?" I said. "Where's your third rod?" So I said, "Well I have got another rod with me but it's folded up, standing there."

I'd got the rod folded in half and elastic banded top and bottom, standing up against a little willow tree but with a boilie on it, as I'd only just wound it in at Savay a couple of hours before. "Ah," he said. "Three rods – gotcha." So I said, "What are you talking about? I'm fishing two rods." He said, "Yeah, but you've got another rod standing there." I said, "Yeah broken in half, not cast out, with elastic bands top and bottom, as per the rule." "No, no, that's not the rule," he said. "It says in the rule book all rods have got to be in a rod holdall." I said, "Excuse me for disagreeing mate, but it doesn't say that in the rule book at all. It just says all rods have got to be packed away, and I've actually called Tony Booker and asked him if folding them up with two elastic bands top and bottom counts as being packed away, and he told me it does." "Oh no, no, I'm not having that," he said. "I'll be bringing this up at the committee meeting. I need to take your number." So I said, "Whatever mate, here's my number," and I showed him my card.

Anyway, I got a letter in the post about a week later saying I was invited along to the next committee meeting, which was in a pub in Rickmansworth, and one of the subjects was going to be my use of three rods down at the Waltonians. So I wrote back and said I didn't use three rods; I'd got another rod in elastic bands, but it was folded up and packed away, and to check the definition of being packed away with Tony Booker, because as far as I was concerned, I hadn't broken any rules, and I wouldn't be attending the committee meeting.

Anyway, Alan Bradley, the guy who I'd fished with the previous year, was now working in Middlesex Angling Centre with Keith Selleck. I happened to be on the phone a few days later to Middlesex Angling ordering a few bits, when Alan Bradley came on the phone, and he said, "I hear you lost your Waltonians ticket, then." So I said, "What do you mean I lost my Waltonians ticket?" So he said, "They were all in here earlier talking about it; you've lost it for using three rods." I said, "What, who was in there earlier?" He said, "They all were, and you're not going to the meeting, so you've lost your ticket for the Waltonians for using three rods." I said, "Bloody hell, I don't believe this lot. When are they gonna leave me alone?"

So I dug the letter out; I hadn't thrown it away. The meeting was the next evening so I thought, right; I'm going to go. I got my best suit, tie and ironed white shirt, and down to the pub I went. The meeting started at 7.00pm, and I was in there at about 7.15pm. I went to the bar and I said "I'm here for the fishing meeting," and I was told, "Oh it's in a room upstairs, first door on the left." So I went up the stairs, knocked on the door, opened it, and you could have heard a pin drop. All the committee were at the head table, with all the head honchos on it, and either side of the room there were tables with the bailiffs and officials of the club all sat there. And guess who they were talking about? Me.

So Graham stood up as chairman and said, "Oh Rob, we were just talking about you." So I turned round to Trevor Willoughby, who was sat on the top table as well, and I said, "That makes a change doesn't it, Trevor, you talking about me?" So Graham said, "Look Rob, now you're here, we want

I'm looking smart.

Veiny again. Superb!

to hear what you've got to say, but can you give us a few minutes? Can you go downstairs and I'll come and get you." So I went downstairs and I was fuming. A few minutes later he came down, took me upstairs, and sat me down at the end of one of the tables, right opposite the guy with the white hair. So Graham stood up and said, "Right, we'll hear the evidence again from our bailiff, Mr So and So, but can we hear what you've got to say, Rob?" So I said, "Well yeah, it was about five o'clock in the afternoon; I'd fished at Savay all weekend, and I had three rods with me. When I arrived, they were broken down in half with boilies attached, and with elastic bands round top and bottom. I'd checked with Tony Booker that this was ok, and he told me it was. I cast two rods out in the lake, and I saw your officials going around the lake. A fish rolled, so I wound one of my rods in and cast to where the fish rolled. With that that guy over there with the white hair came flying into my swim, started marching around in the margins, and accused me of using three rods because I'd got a rod broken down in elastic bands. I told him I wasn't, and he said I should get a rod holdall."

With that he shouted across the room, "Well you should get a rod holdall." I said, "Look, you can see how rude he is! When he was down there he said to me I'd got to buy a rod holdall, but I don't use a rod holdall." I said, "He was really rude to me, and I think he should apologise." With that he stood up and said, "Apologise? Apologise? I'll come over there and give you an apology in a minute!" and started shaking his fist at me. So I stood up and said, "Look, I thought I'd come to a civilized meeting where I was going to talk about being wrongly accused of using three rods. He searched my swim from top to bottom, and there weren't three rods cast out in the swim, and he was rude, and now he's threatening to punch me." So Graham said, "Ok, ok, alright, calm down, calm down. Rob, step outside the door for a minute. We're going to have a little chat, and we're going to come to a decision."

So I stood outside the door, and a few seconds later Graham came through the door to talk to me. He said, "Cor, dear oh dear, mate. You could do without this, couldn't you?" I said, "I know, I haven't done anything." He said, "Look don't worry, we'll sort it out. Just wait here a moment and we'll go back and make a decision." He walked back in, and I'd got my ear to the door. He sat down at the top of the table and he said, "Right, well I think he's guilty." My hair stood up on end, and this after he'd come out and told me that I don't need the hassle, and that it would all be sorted out. He went straight back in and stuck the knife between my shoulder blades. I just couldn't believe it.

Anyway, they talked about it for a few minutes more, but they obviously realised they hadn't got any evidence, and that if they wanted to get me out they'd have to get a better reason than that. So I came back into the meeting and Graham said, "Well look, we've talked about it, and there doesn't seem to be any evidence that you had three rods out, so just make sure that you don't break any more rules. We will be watching you and we're just letting you know to be very careful down there." I went out the door and I thought to myself, well I've still got my ticket, but I'd better make the best of it, because the first little thing, I just knew they were going to have me out.

Anyway, about this time I was writing my first book, Tiger Bay, and I knew that there was a publicity ban on the North Harrow Waltonians, but I really wanted to write about my seasons down there. I wondered how I could go about it without breaking a rule, so I spoke to a few friends and they said, well if you make up a fictitious name so that nobody could possibly guess the whereabouts of the fishery, you've got to be ok. So I

Making the most of it before I get the chop.

decided to call the lake Springwood, thinking that no one would ever put two and two together unless they knew I was fishing at the North Harrow Waltonians and guess the name of the venue. I asked Lee Jackson and Martin Locke if they would write guest chapters in my book, and told them that as it was a no-publicity venue, they to should change the name to Springwood in their articles. A week after the book came out, I had a call from the club telling me that my ticket had been revoked, and that I now faced a life ban from the North Harrow Waltonians for breaking the no-publicity rule and naming the water. Furthermore, my friends Martin Locke and Lee Jackson would receive a ban of, I believe, six months from the venue for writing their guest chapters in my book.

I was so disappointed... I'm not going to say heartbroken, because I wouldn't want to give them the satisfaction of thinking that they had really hurt me, but they had. They'd taken away somewhere that I loved to be, somewhere that was a very difficult water to fish with its night fishing ban and its intricate lakebed, somewhere I'd worked hard to catch the fish, and earned every fish that I caught. I'd not broken the rules that they said I had, but I was just so gutted that I accepted the ban without a fuss. Lee and Martin both spoke to me and said, "Thanks a lot mate; you've dropped us right in it," so I could have easily fallen out with two of my best friends over it too. Luckily they were good friends and we didn't fall out about it, but it was horrible.

Bearing in mind that it was back in 1984 or 1985, I can't remember exactly, it's unbelievable that they've never come back to me in those 25 years and said, "Well you've served your sentence; you've done your time, and we'll offer you your ticket back." So I'm still serving a life ban from this water 25 years later, and I really didn't even break a rule. In fact I was having a conversation about it with Lee Jackson in August of 2010, telling him that I was going to write a few of the things that had happened to me, a few of the home truths that had gone on in my fishing. He said how wrong it all was, and if I had taken them to court, to a judge and a jury I'd called it Springwood, not the North Harrow Waltonians, so how on earth had I given away the whereabouts? They'd have laughed it out of court, and I'd have probably still had my ticket. But they wanted me out, and if it wasn't going be for that, it was going be for something else. I'd only got to be one minute late up to the car park and not off the venue by the allocated time, and my ticket would have been cut in half, and my time would have been ended on Harrow anyway.

So that was a sad ending to one of the most enjoyable bits of fishing in my life. There are very few places you can go to that are an unknown, where every fish and every weight is not known before you catch it, but this was my time to christen a few of the country's most beautiful carp... The Veiny One, Dearman's, the Plate, Moonscale, but they're all long gone now I suppose. I think the venue has gone on to produce two different 60lb-plus carp, no end of 40lb'ers, and some 50lb'ers too. And just as a last little stab between the shoulder blades for me, the following year after getting me out of the club, they relaxed the no-publicity rule. They didn't do away with it completely, but what they decided was that anybody who wrote about the North Harrow Waltonians Angling Club in an article or in Carp-Talk to promote a bait or some tackle or something had to pay the club some money. I think it was £50 every time it was named. So there you go – a few months later the rule didn't even exist, but they still never came back to me and said, "Rob, we've made a mistake, maybe we was a bit harsh with you. Sorry about that mate, but you caught too many fish." Story of my life...

Chapter 4
A Breath of Fresh Air —
Problems Left Behind Me?

"The Savay rulebook was – what Peter says, goes."

Fishing Savay again was like a breath of fresh air after all the problems at the North Harrow Waltonians. I've never been a political angler and for that matter not a massive rule breaker either, but fishing places like the North Harrow Waltonians you just couldn't escape it. I'm an angler who likes to go fishing, catch some fish, have a drink with his friends, catch up with what's been going on with his mates and come home having had a good weekend, not to be on the bank bitching and backbiting about what someone else is doing and whether somebody should be doing this or not and what rules they've been breaking; that's never been me. So going to Savay again after all that trouble at Waltonians really did take a weight off my shoulders, and it was like I was fishing it with a clear head.

The thing with Savay that was different to the Waltonians was not that there weren't any rules, or that it wasn't strict; it was. Savay was stricter than the North Harrow Waltonians due to one man – Peter Broxup. The rulebook, which was 100 pages long for the North Harrow Waltonians, didn't exist on Savay – the Savay rulebook was "what Peter says goes". If Peter said you could do it, you could do it, and if Peter said you couldn't do it, you couldn't do it, and that was that. Now if you wanted to break those rules at Savay and face the consequences from Peter Broxup, then you needed to be a great man because he didn't suffer fools lightly, and he ran a very tight ship. He was well liked, don't get me wrong; he wasn't a raging tyrant that everybody hated, he was a raging tyrant that everybody liked and respected for what he did at Savay. He kept the place immaculate; the syndicate was well groomed, and the people who joined were the right people. By that I mean when I was on Savay there were people on the waiting list for ten years, and they would just never get in because in Peter's view, or in the view of the other people who had a say in who was a possible syndicate member, people like Roger Smith and John Harry, they weren't the right people. So, they kept a waiting list but if you were one of the ones they wanted in, you could more or less get straight in. I've got to say, Peter and his crew were pretty good judges of people and the syndicate got on really well together.

I certainly found that one of the most fantastic things about fishing Savay was the guys who were on there. The guys in the two syndicate rotas, the Looneys and the Toads were all really nice. The Looneys were the pub goers, the beer monsters, and the guys who didn't take it all too seriously. Don't get me wrong; they wanted to catch fish, believe me, and would go to most lengths to get them, but they wanted to have a good time too, whereas the Toad rota guys were picked because they were very, very dedicated. You wouldn't get them up to the pub, except maybe for a

Christmas drink or something, but certainly not every week like us. We fished it mainly at the weekends; it was a week on, week off syndicate rota, so twice a month we were down there from Friday after work until Sunday afternoon, and we made the best of the pub times while we were there. The rotas merged in November and you could go every week.

I've got to tell you that there were certain practices that went on down there that are certainly frowned upon in today's carp fishing and certainly not something that I'm proud of, but they are just something that happened, and for the sake of this chapter, I think these things need to be mentioned. This chapter's not all about the fish captures that I had at Savay, because I've already written books on Savay – Tiger Bay and Fox Pool both had Savay written right across them. I mean Tiger Bay was virtually all about Savay, and the fact that I'd used tiger nuts in the North Bay. I mean that's what that title is all about, and I've got to tell you it didn't go down too well with Peter Broxup when I brought that book out. He pulled me to one side and said, "Are you f***ing taking the pee out of me?" Nobody to this day knows how I did it, but I will tell you about it and some of the other practices that went on down there. Thankfully, those days have gone and we care so much more about the fish these days so these sorts of things don't happen, but let's get things into perspective…

Years ago when Richard Walker was the man, the carp angler of the day, and he was fishing at Redmire Pool, all sorts of things went on down there that we wouldn't do today, and with other big fish caught before and even after his time. For a start no one had unhooking mats, which weren't invented until the mid-80s. I'd been fishing for carp for ten years by then, and when you caught a fish you looked around for a nice soft bit of grass to put it on. You never took a cushion to lay it on, and of course nor did the top anglers of the early days. In fact on occasion they never had scales or anything and would end up taking the carp somewhere to get it weighed. I remember a story from Redmire Pool where a record carp was taken to the railway station to be weighed, and in fact Walker's record, Clarissa the 44lb common, was taken from the lake when he caught it and put in the zoo. I mean people would go absolutely crazy these days if you did these sorts of things.

There' another story concerning an earlier record carp a 26 caught from Mapperley Reservoir by a guy who took it home across the handlebars of his pushbike. So it hasn't always been very fair on the carp, and it's only as time has gone on that carp anglers have taken a lot more care and used a lot more sense when handling and moving carp from one place to another. Unfortunately in years gone by the damage must have been incredible to

Maylin's Pads and the Mean Machine

Savay 1983.

Looking across the canal bank to John Harry's bivvy on the Ruislip Island, 1983.

(John Harry, 30 years a Savay man.

We would soon become 'The Famous Five'.

Hutchy's 'Thick Head Fish', the start of a flurry of 30-pluses.

Steve Alcott and Ian Guy do the honours.

Steve's Savay record.

Angling Times 1986.

Steve and I, twins divided at birth.

Gerrards Cross ticket 1986.

Roger Smith in action in the Gravely

these fish that were carted backwards and forwards to railways stations etc. At Savay there was certainly none of that going on, but it was the first water that I ever fished where the practice of leaving rods unattended was fairly commonplace. It's a very touchy subject, and I'm certainly not going to get into naming names.

I'm thankful that those days are over, but it went on, and it was spoken about in hushed voices. It was fairly lighthearted, a bit of a joke at the time,

35-plus and a new PB.

but obviously very serious for the fish. It's not something that we'd do these days, but leaving the rods out was something that went on down there. But that procedure wasn't really breaking any rules; it was a sort of an unwritten rule that it went on at night and a blind eye was turned to it. I think if anyone was caught doing it then there would be a severe reprimand, but certainly no one was caught doing it because no one was looking for it.

The trouble is, when these sorts of practices go on, people then begin to think that everybody is doing it, and everybody is catching fish doing it, and that certainly wasn't the case. Not everybody was doing it, and if there were any fish caught doing it, then it was a very small number. I mean it's 30 years ago now since I was down there and I can't really remember anybody catching one with a rod that was left with the bait out, but needless to say, for the purpose of this piece, I wanted to mention that it went on, but I'm glad that it doesn't go on any more.

A rule that I certainly broke was the use of tiger nuts when they were banned. I'm not sure about any others, because I think they were all a bit too scared of Peter. Not that I wasn't scared, but I wanted to take my chance. Dickie Cauldwell, Martin Locke and Dave Whibley began baiting up Savay with tigers in the early 80s, and I think I started using them around about 84 or 85, and the carp wanted them to the exclusion of anything else. You could put as many boilies out as you wanted, but bait a patch of tigers in the edge or under a bush, or even further out, and they were on them. Having caught a few fish on them and quite a few other people did as well, suddenly to find that there was a rule that there were to be no particles on Savay other than sweetcorn and hemp (which weren't bad ones by the way), but no peanuts, no tigers, and no more peas or beans that had been popular there in the past was a bit of a headbanger to be honest, and I went back to boilies.

I fished them for a few weeks but the bites just totally dried up, so I had to come up with a plan. It's a difficult one with tigers because of the nature of the bait. If a carp expels a tiger nut in any form through its vent, it will be seen by people at the unhooking mat stage. So in layman's terms, if they poo out tiger nuts then they're going to know that they were feeding on tiger nuts, and you're captured, so that's something you've got to be careful of. If you intend to catapult tiger nuts out into the lake, you've got to be 100% certain that none of these end up on the bank. You know, baits drop out of the catapult pouch or ping out at an awkward angle. If Peter Broxup came walking along and saw two or three tiger nuts in the shallow water in your margins, your feet would not touch the ground, and I didn't want to come up against his vengeance, so I came up with a cunning plan...

The captor returns.

'The Tooth' with Popeye.

'Harper the Carper'.

Colne bank winter.

Lockey on the Colne bank.

Roger writes up his diary on the canal bank, 1983.

Kerry and The Beast.

Tiger nut stroke puller.

Trotter and Popeye.

Dave Whibley, canal bank monster!

Savay football team, 1983.

I bought myself a half-hundredweight sack of tiger nuts, cooked them all up and froze them in bags of about a pound. You don't need many tiger nuts to bait up and to get the fish going on them, and a pound for a night session was about right. I decided to concentrate on the North Bay, one, because it was close to the car park, and I intended doing just nights and go off to work so there would be little walking involved, and two, that I had already caught a couple out of there on tigers, so it was just a matter of waiting for them to turn up. Savay was a big lake and the fish went round the lake, so they weren't always in the North Bay. They'd be here there and everywhere, but during the course of a few days, there'd be fish turning up in the North Bay and they would find the little patches of tigers sitting out there. They weren't going to go off or anything; tigers just sit on the bottom until the carp come along, unlike boilies that would go off after a time and then pop to the surface leaving a foul smelling, poisonous bait in the lake. Tigers weren't like that; tigers just sat there on the bottom as tigers until carp came along.

One of Savay's finest.

So I decided that the first swim up the Alcatraz arm of the North Bay would be my plot if you like; in fact it became known, much to the annoyance of Peter Broxup by the way, as Maylin's Pads. Now the swim itself I've described in my other books, but just for the purpose of this piece, was basically boards going out over the top of a reed bed probably 20yds deep to the water's edge, then large patches of lily pads in this bay area of the lake, which was fairly shallow and quite silty – perfect for tigers.

So what I decided to do was never catapult a tiger from the bank because the water was quite shallow in the edge. Rather than raise any suspicions that I'd been wading, I never ever took chest waders either, but simply stripped off down to my underpants when I arrived at the lake in the evening just on dark, waded out to just below my chin carrying the tigers in a plastic bag and catapulted them out in three areas – to my right against the far sets of pads, almost straight out up against the left hand edge of the pads nearest to me, and another patch of tigers out in open water over towards the corner of the lake opposite me. They were easy spots to catapult tigers to as I used shadows on the lake from trees on the far horizon, and these dark patches from some round shaped trees opposite me offered the perfect baiting areas every evening that I came down.

It was a mad rush to get down to Savay and to get into the North Bay without letting anybody know that I was there because it wouldn't have been far off pub time by then and people would soon be coming down ready to go to the pub. The guys who were fishing there midweek visited the pub every evening, not just the weekends, and they would have been Roger and Kerry and a few of the other full-timers. I wasn't a full-timer but I was making the most of doing a few evenings down there after work and staying until the following morning because my son Ashleigh was about to be born, and I knew that once he was born my fishing time would be cut, plus I wanted to give the tigers one last go down in the North Bay. So, rushing to the swim, trying not to alert anybody that I was there, I'd strip off down to my underpants and get straight into the lake, and this was October/November time so it wasn't pleasant. I'd wade out as far as I could and then catapult three patches of tigers accurately.

Now in amongst the pound of tigers I put in about 8oz of tiny boilies that I rolled – tiny little fishmeal boilies with a salmon oil and meat extract flavour. I rolled a big batch of these up and then split them between the tigers so it wasn't all tigers that I put out there. It was these little boilies that I was going to actually use as hookbaits, as using a tiger I was obviously going to get captured. Someone would come along as I was playing a fish and there would be a tiger hanging out of its mouth, and the next minute there'd be a size 12 boot straight up my backside and I'd be in the lake, so there was none of that. I had to use these little fishmeal pop-ups and kept the flavour down to a minimum. I didn't want a big attractor out there because I think that that would have been avoided by the carp; I wanted something that would just be eaten by accident while they were out there eating the tigers amongst all the silt, crunching up the tigers and also getting the occasional tiny boilie in there with very little flavour in it. The first time I tried it, I caught and I went on to catch five thirties from the North Bay and a few others as well. You'll have to read the other books for the stories, some of them quite amusing, but now you know the full story around what actually went on down there.

There's also the fantastic story of the Mad Knifeman of the North Bay. If you haven't read that, it's perfectly true, but a great story. I went on to catch about 12 or 15 fish, which made me top rod on the Looney rota that year by quite a distance. I think the nearest to me was maybe Kerry or even

Son of Popeye.

Soon to be Rompey's 40-plus bloater.

Kerry with son of Popeye.

Winter 20.

Canal bank, three in a day.

My favourite Savay carp.

Rigby the carp.

Steve with Son of Popeye.

Honourary and Fox Pool permit.

Bruce, Steve and Phil contemplate the freeze...

...while I winkle one out.

Off to pastures new.

Dave Whibley in action at Fox Pool.

Dickie Cauldwell on about eight fish, so I more or less doubled what the next rod to me caught. I've always been the same; if I'm onto a winning combination, I will go to any lengths to use it, even risking life and limb at Savay and the wrath of Peter Broxup. When I arrived at the lake, had he searched me and I'd had tigers on me, my feet would not have touched the ground. But within five minutes of arriving at the lake, I was naked and wet, but there were no tigers anywhere to be seen; they were out in the lake.

Luckily most of the fish that I caught were at night, and the odd one on the unhooking mat was never seen. I was suspected by everybody, all the Looney rota, my good friends, Steve Alcott, Dave Whibley, Martin Locke; they all suspected me of using them, but I stuck to my story, "No I'm using tiny little boilies – here they are." I was showing them the pop-ups I was catching them on; these little tiny fishmeal boilies with hardly any flavour, sitting out there amongst about ten pouches of tiger nuts, and they were just getting eaten up with the tigers. I did do a few heads in down there I've got to admit, so sorry about that, lads, but you know the truth now. Everybody suspected me of it, including Pete Broxup, but no one ever caught me doing it, and that was the main thing – that was how I kept my ticket for as long as I did.

We had some tremendous times down at Savay, and I formed some lifelong friendships. We had an absolute whale of the time down there; we would take extra sets of clothes with us as we set off for the weekend, and there was more attention paid to where we were going out on a Friday and Saturday night than where we were actually bothering to fish. Very often the fishing was decided by who was there first – if Steve Alcott or I were set up on the Canal Bank, the other lads would turn up later and go either side so we had a social for the weekend. If one of us was round on the Colne Bank then that's where we'd all end up and so on and so forth, but we had some fantastic times down there. At that time, the Round Island, the syndicate island, which became Peter's island in later years, was actually open to the syndicate, and you could spend the weekend on the island there and it was great; it was like being shipwrecked. Steve Alcott and I had some great fun on there on numerous occasions, as we did everywhere else.

Some terrible things happened at Savay while we were there, and some of our good friends passed away. Bob Jones, Roger Smith's good buddy passed away through alcohol abuse, and Keith Sellick and a guy called Clive Rigsby both drowned. Although I wasn't there at the time, the story of the drowning was relayed to me by someone else who was in the boat at the time, Martin Locke. It is a truly horrific tale but something that I want to mention here, as a warning really to all the guys who think that they're bulletproof and go out in boats without lifejackets, and without even being able to swim in some cases, and that was of course the case with Rigsby.

The boat was out on the Round Island, and the guys were doing some work down there, or some sort of bank clearance or something. Anyway, they all ended up in the boat on the way back, including Keith Sellick, Martin Locke and Rigsby and a few others. Martin explained that they were making a good pace back, when suddenly the front of the boat dipped under the water, and within a second the boat was totally full of water and everybody was floundering around with some distance to go before the shore. Rigsby, the poor man, was lost fairly quickly despite the efforts of some of the others trying to save him. He couldn't swim at all; he had no life jacket and his clothes soon became heavy weights pulling him down. With 100yds or more still to the shore, people were worried about their own lives, and couldn't devote the time necessary to somebody thrashing around who had no real chance of getting back to the side.

The story of Keith Sellick is even more sad... The other guys in the boat had got back to the shore by now, and Keith, who was a good swimmer, was making steady progress. He was the last one coming in and the rest of the guy were on the shore saying, "Come on, Keith, only a few more yards to go mate, you're nearly there, you're nearly there." Keith was looking up, nodding and saying he was on his way, but then within a couple of yards of the bank, suddenly he sank below the surface. Whether he'd had a cramp or a heart attack or just lost energy and lost his last gasp of air, we'll never know, but he sank. The guys jumped back in and dived down but they couldn't see him, and everyone was screaming and shouting, "Where is he? He's got to be there somewhere!" But because the currents are strong in those big gravel pits he was soon swept away from the spot where he went down, and I believe it took the police divers another 24 hours at least to find his body, which was some distance away from where it went down. An immense tragedy – two such well liked people in the syndicate who left families behind, and it shocked the carp world at the time.

I really had hoped that people would learn from this lesson, yet some years later there were a couple of guys who drowned after getting in trouble in a boat at Wraysbury one New Year's Eve. It just goes to show what a fine thread of life we have, and there but for the grace of God go I, because I've been out in that boat at Savay many a time, sometimes in the middle of the night, and I'm ashamed to say not always with a lifejacket on, and I'm not a brilliant swimmer either. I don't know how I would have coped with full winter clothing going in the middle of Savay in the winter. I certainly had no lifejacket on a couple of occasions that I've gone out there, and I'm

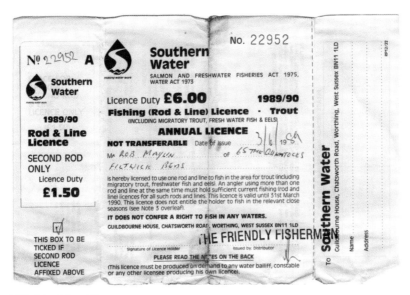

1989-90 – £6 rod licence.

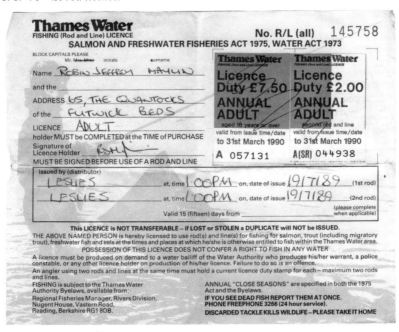

1990-91 – £7.50 rod licence.

Yateley ticket for
The Copse.

GET that tackle out! It's even possible to catch carp in Winter . . . as Rob Maylin shows here.

Rob tells you how to tackle the carp at this time of year on Page 8, where he explains that, even with snow on the banks, carp will cruise around looking for food. And there's no need

to camp out overnight.

Every year big catches are made over Christmas and New Year, and this season it may be your turn. So whether your favourite species is roach, chub, dace, perch . . . or even carp, there's no need to stop fishing. Get out there and give it a try. You could end up with a fish like Rob's.

Front page Angling Times with one in the snow, 1986.

Jack.

Kerry catches Bazil first trip.

A classic.

Trotter and Shoulders.

Angling Times floater record.

Bungalow bank celebrations.

Floating fishing lesson.

pleased to tell you that that won't happen again. If I'm out in a boat now I've got a good lifesaving vest on me, and I always carry a couple with me when I'm fishing now. So as you can see, along with the many really happy times I had down at Savay, there were some occasions of great sadness too.

I fished Savay for two years on the syndicate and one year on day ticket. It all came to an end in 1986 after the hurricanes had struck across Britain and caused devastation down at Savay, and most of Britain for that matter. Quite a few trees had fallen down

Holsten Ray and Shakey Dell.

across the path at Savay, and on this particular weekend Steve Alcott, Phil Harper, Ian Guy, Dave Whibley and I had found ourselves round on the Colne Bank. The Colne Bank at Savay was the long walk bank; it took you about three quarters of an hour to walk round there from the car park, and if you intended to fish round there it was highly unlikely you'd get all of your tackle for a weekend round there in one go. It normally took two trips so you would bring round the bulk of the stuff and have a look round to see if you could see any fish on the Colne Bank. Whether we fished round there or not depended on whether the fish were there or whether fish had been caught there during the week by other anglers. There were certain times of the year when the Colne was better than other areas. We didn't fish the Colne Bank to the exclusion of the other banks, but certainly at certain times of the year it was the favourite area, and autumn, early winter was one of those times. So, after struggling to get our gear round there, we all found ourselves bivvied up on the Colne Bank for the weekend.

Come Sunday afternoon when we were thinking about the horrendous walk back to the car park – two trips through the jungle of fallen trees around the paths – we had a visitor come across by ferry from the Ruislip Island, the Long Island that was in front of you. There was a system of ferries on there that were for use by the bailiffs and for the Ruislip members, and it was none other than Keith Sellick, the guy who unfortunately died in the drowning accident some years later. He came round to see how we were doing and to say how hard it was going to be for us to get back round to the car park.

Now Keith was Peter Broxup's best friend; they fished together, they socialised together, and I think their wives were friendly. Keith owned Middlesex Angling Centre, which was the local tackle shop where Peter and all the rest of the guys from Savay shopped for their tackle and bait, and of course he had a great relationship with Keith and they were great friends.

Anyway Keith came over to me and said, "Look, I will leave the raft gates open and the padlock's open for you guys to get back to the car park." Packing up normally consisted of two trips round, each one taking 45 minutes, but Keith doing that would cut packing up and getting back to the car park down to ten minutes as opposed to over three hours. I said to Keith, "Are you sure you want to do this, because you know what Peter's like?" "No, no, no, that's all right; he won't find out. We'll keep it quiet obviously, just go across on the ferry and good luck to you." So I told the other guys what he had said and everybody was made up, saying, "Yeah, yeah, we'll do that – thanks a lot, Keith."

So Keith pulled the ferry back to the Long Island from the Colne Bank but left the lock undone so that we could pull the ferry back to us and get all our tackle on there. You could go by ferry to the Long Island and then you could get on another ferry and go across to Alcatraz, which is where the car park is. So it was very, very quick compared to hours of trudging backwards and forwards with a heavy tackle. Nothing had to be carried; it all just sat on the ferry and was pulled across.

We had to be off there at four o'clock in the afternoon so I think it was probably about 3.30pm, and everyone had packed up. We all got our gear on the ferry, all excited and giggling, larking around, pushing each other, and we pulled ourselves quietly across to the Long Island. We had a good look around when we got there, as no one was around – no Peter, no John Harry, no bailiffs, just Martin Locke. He was on the Canal Bank so somebody shouted across "Oi, Martin," and Martin waved and we all waved back, and we started singing, "Row, row, row your boat gently down the stream, merrily, merrily, merrily, merrily, life is but a dream…" and we were all pulling on the rope in unison, all five of us, the Famous Five as we were going to be called quite shortly. We were pulling ourselves across, singing to Martin, and all of a sudden Martin didn't look very happy. He was shaking his fist in the air, screaming something at the top of his voice and jumping up and down, throwing stuff all over the place. I said to Steve Alcott, "That is Martin over there, isn't it?" and Steve said, "Oh my God, it's not Martin it's Broxup... Shit!"

Anyway we were quiet then, but we'd done the damage. We got off the ferry, and we'd made our minds up not to drop Keith in it at any cost. If we mentioned that Keith had left the gate open, he would be losing his ticket,

Shoulders at last.

Action in the trees.

The exquisite Heart Tail.

Drained and done.

Dude, where's my car?

Steve scores at last...

...then does it again!

and we didn't want that at all. Anyway, there was this cracking, like trees were falling down as something made its way through the jungle. It was like King Kong was coming, snapping trees off at the base as it was coming through the wooded area of the North Bay, and it was indeed a huge silverback – Pete Broxup. I'd never seen anything as red as his face in my life, and steam was coming out of his ears and the top of his shirt collar; he was absolutely fuming. "Give me your tickets," was all he said, and he grabbed all five of the tickets. "Right now, off my water!" That was it, and we all stood there in amazement.

It was a very, very sad time; I mean we were absolutely gutted, the lot of us – devastated. Savay was our life, and we loved it there. We'd had amazing times there over the years, summer and winter; we knew the banks like the backs of our hands, and we knew the swims so well. I mean honestly, we'd have probably been there for another ten years if we hadn't have been chucked out at that particular time.

We felt pleased that we hadn't dropped Keith Sellick in it. As I mentioned earlier, he did die some years later, and there's an end to this story that makes it a bit weird really I suppose. Peter was in a foul temper and that afternoon, he said to me, "From now on, you don't exist. Don't ever say one word to me again," so I said, "Ok."

I had written Tiger Bay by then, and he obviously knew that I'd had one over on him, and he was pleased to get me out of the syndicate. John Harry told me 20 years later, when I did a revised chapter in his Savay book, that Peter was really cross because he had to be fair that day and remove everybody's tickets who were on the ferry. Really it was mine that he wanted because of the Tiger Bay episode, and he felt like I'd already had one chance and this was my second chance that I'd blown, whereas the others, this was their first chance. But he had to chuck out Steve Alcott and Phil Harper, and he really liked those guys; they were mates.

So that was one of the reasons he was in such a bad temper. I actually told John Harry in his kitchen down at Ruislip that day for the first time what actually happened about Keith Sellick leaving the gate open, and John said, "Peter never knew that, you know." I said "No, no, I know he didn't; we never ever told anyone. In fact you're the first person we've told, even though Keith's dead. We could have said, but what was the point anyway?" And John said, "Well maybe you should have said, as that would have changed things for you." But at what cost – Keith Sellick losing his ticket for a lifetime for doing something nice for us? I mean we're not that sort of people, so we never dropped Keith in it, and even after he died, there didn't seem lot of point in saying, "Well hold on a minute, Peter, perhaps you should know that it was your best pal that gave us permission to use the raft that day and we were only doing what we were offered really, the same as anybody would."

Of course Peter wouldn't have heard that from me, in fact I didn't see Peter Broxup for about another ten years. I happened to be walking up Moorhall Road towards the café, the road that Savay and Harefield are on, and walking down the road on my the side was Peter Broxup. I hadn't seen Peter for years, and in the intervening years of course Keith Sellick had died. Keith was a good friend of both of ours, and I did want to say to Peter how sorry I was for Keith's sad death. As he approached me he actually looked up at me and I said, "Peter, I'm so sorry to hear about Keith," and he looked at me with such hatred in his face, and he said, "I thought I told you not to f***ing speak to me again," and that was ten years later!!!

So Peter never ever forgave me for using tiger nuts or whatever. It was a shame really, as I really respected Pete; I thought he was a good guy on there, very fair. I'd broken the rules and got caught and I had to face my punishment. But I wish that as time had gone on that we could have made amends. He wasn't one to forgive unfortunately, and even just before he died in 2007, Tim Paisley came up to me at one of the shows and said, "Look, you, Rod Hutchinson and Peter Broxup are all here today, how would you feel about all going up on the stage and having a chat about Savay?" Rod had fished it in the 70s and early 80s; I had fished it in the 80s and Broxup had fished it in the 90s up to the 2000s, so between the three of us we'd covered the last 40 years of fishing on Savay. It would have been a great thing to have recorded the history of Savay over that period of time with three anglers who had done well there. I don't want to put my name in the frame for dominating the venue; I didn't dominate the venue, but I was top rod on my syndicate when I was on there, and Rod was when he was on there, and Broxup was when he was on there. So you know, we had caught the most fish certainly through those eras. Of course Rod agreed, and I said to Paisley, "I doubt very much Pete Broxup will do it because of me," and he said, "Oh no, Pete's alright, I'll talk him round." He came back five minutes later and said, "No, you're right; Pete won't do it."

So right up until his death he held a grudge, and you know all I've got to

Bookers, RIP.

A rare brace.

say to Peter is, "Rest in peace, mate. I'm sorry you and I couldn't have been friends because I really did respect you for what you did on Savay and the way you ran the place." Not that it's gone downhill or anything; I don't think it has. It's obviously been taken over now; it's been bought by a guy called Tom Banks, and I think he does a little bit of bailiffing on there. There's a small syndicate on there still, and John Harry of course is the head bailiff. You don't really hear a lot about Savay these days, but of course when I fished it and Rod for that matter, we publicised it to a great extent. Rod's first and second books were set at Savay, and when The Carp Strikes Back came out, I remember reading that book on about three or four occasions and thinking it was absolutely fantastic.

Of course Tiger Bay, my first book, was mostly about Savay, and I know how important that book has been to people throughout the years. I've had people come up to me over the years, saying, "It got me into carp fishing," or, "It saved my life." One bloke said he had read it in prison a couple of times. For whatever reason it was written, I certainly never wrote it with the intention of taking the piss out of Peter or anybody at Savay, and it

I found the key.

stands now as a book that most carp anglers have read and enjoyed.

Just one final tale I have remembered before I move on. One of the highlights of an amazing era on Savay. As I told you, the weeks were split week on, week off for the two rotas and 4pm was the change over time on Sundays. So, as a loony, I had to be off by 4pm as the Toad rota had started. But we all used to hang it out for five to tem minutes. Why? To catch one on the other rota of course. To put two fingers up to the Toads. In the winter of 1985 I achieved the impossible by catching one 31 pounder at 4.05pm. I had caught one on the Toad rota, what a result. I had three portions of mushrooms for breakfast. The fish was 'Rigsby's fish' named of course after poor old Clive who drowned so tragically in the Cottage Bay. I'd like to think Clive had a good old smile about that one, wherever he is now. RIP.

So that was it; we were out, and we couldn't believe it. We were chucked out of Savay. I'd never heard of anybody getting chucked out of there; I mean you've really got to do something terrible to get chucked out. Maybe it would just be a three-month ban or a six-month ban, but it didn't look like that was going to be the case. However, even if rumours aren't true,

Dave and The Lady.

mud sticks, and I began to get a bit of a bad name, and my nickname suddenly became Rob Mayhem, a guy who was getting banned from every water in the Colne Valley quicker than he was catching the fish, but I hadn't really done anything wrong. I mean the Harrow thing which started it all off was just from writing the chapter on Springwood, which had never crossed the lines of disclosing where the venue was and breaking the no publicity rule, but that's why I lost my ticket, and Savay too. I remember the headline in the Angling Times that week was 'Famous Five lose their tickets at Savay for break-dancing on a boat', as somehow it got round that we were all dancing on this raft.

I was getting a bad name, and I didn't like it particularly. I've never been a rule breaker in the past; I've never been one to cause problems to anybody anyway, and this was on two waters. In fact Broxup talked to me earlier that year to say that he had had a call from John Stent, who ran Boyer Fisheries at the time. I don't think Pete Broxup particularly liked John Stent from what I could gather, but John Stent said, "If you have any trouble with these boys, just give me their names and I'll ban them from all my waters as well." So Broxup told him 'f' off I think and said, "Don't be ridiculous; they haven't done anything on your waters." He didn't suffer fools lightly, and I don't really think he appreciated that at all from John Stent. Actually John Stent went on to be a good friend of mine. I've got to say that he'd probably heard the rumours and thought, well, if that's going to be the case I don't want them on Boyer Waters, and fair enough. But when he actually met all the guys... I fished a long time down on Farlows and then Harefield, another one of his lakes, and I always found him to be ok and to be honest, and we got on pretty well together. But quite easily, we could have lost all the Redlands lakes that Peter ran, and if Peter had have been vindictive, lost all the Boyer Lakes as well, and I would have never fished Farlows or Harefield. So you know, that just showed the sort of character that Broxup had anyway.

So we chatted on the phone, 'we' meaning Steve, Phil, me etc, and decided that we would stick together and take on the world, and that the first place we'd go and annihilate was Fox Pool, sometimes known as Staines, sometimes known as Longfield, but certainly a water that we all fancied having a go on. It wasn't a circuit water by any means; it wasn't a water that people had written loads about, unlike Savay that had appeared in numerous publications from the Angling Times right through all the carp fishing magazines. It was on the front cover of the Carp Society issue number 1 with Mike Wilson, and it had had quite a lot of publicity over the years. Longfield hadn't, and most of the guys who had been around for a while had been on there at various times – Pete Springate, Kevin Maddocks, Richie McDonald had all had a little go, and the fish were quite amazing; they were very, very big for that time.

Jack was the biggest fish in the lake, which was coming out at around about 42lb, and there were probably half a dozen other fish of 35lb-plus in there. At the time the biggest fish in Savay was probably around about 35lb, maybe 38lb, but certainly not 40lb. It was some years later before it did a forty; in fact the first forties that came out of there were caught by Albert Romp and Max Cottis. I think Max caught the first one, and then Albert caught caught Max's fish and another one, and they were bloated thirties. In fact they were the same fish that I had caught in the North Bay that autumn on the tigers, and you will see them in my book at around about 32-33lb, and then in Albert's arms about 12lb bigger, but they bloated up and died.

But these fish in Staines were proper history fish – some originals and others from neighbouring lakes that for one reason or another had to have the fish taken out, Yeoveney was one of these of course, just down the road from Longfield – that immaculate brace that Pete Springate shocked the carp world with. Both of those fish ended up in Fox Pool, although I believe one of them, the fatter one of the two, was actually taken out and put into Wraysbury at some stage of its life and then not seen again. But this is where we decided to go.

We were in a strange frame of mind, unlike anything that I've ever felt like before. I think the word would be 'angry' if I were to put any label on it. We were all really angry about what had happened at Savay, and it affected us in our fishing in those couple of seasons we had at Longfield in that we had this angry vibe about us, like we were young men who had been wronged in some way. I think that's how we felt – that we hadn't deserved the punishment that we had received. After all, Keith offered to let us go across on the raft, and we now found ourselves fishing somewhere else. However, it was a fantastic place to fish, and in fact it grew in my heart to such an extent that it's probably my favourite venue I have ever fished. Nowhere I'd ever fished gave me the buzz that that place did – just driving down the track to the lake gave me an amazing buzz.

But we also had this sort of arrogance about us as well that we were the Famous Five; we were going to be famous. We weren't actually famous at the time; we became famous really for getting banned from Savay, not for our captures, but our captures were to take over and become the reason why we were famous, because we went from water to water as a group, just obliterating the place, catching everything in our paths. Because there were a few of us, even if a couple of the guys weren't catching, there was always something being caught and we were always in the headlines for something, and if you're in the headlines enough, soon you become a sort of a household name and that's what happened with us really.

At this time Leisure Sport as it was known, the controlling club for Fox Pool, was run by a lovely old guy called Jack Ashford and he and I became... I wouldn't say friends, but we had a mutual respect for each other. He'd obviously heard about us and we didn't want to go upsetting the applecart when we went down there, although we were who we were and we weren't going to change. We went down there with the same attitudes and the same view on how we fished – 'catching them on our own terms' I think was the phrase we used a lot at that time to justify the amount of time that we spent away from the lake in the nearby Indian restaurants and pubs. That was our motto, and we didn't have to be there 24 hours a day. We would turn up when we wanted and catch them, again all part of this arrogance thing that I was talking about.

But we did, in all fairness, do very well between us at Fox Pool. Dave Whibley had been doing very well at Savay before we got banned, using an ultra spice protein pop-up mix that he had formulated. He caught several fish out of Savay and went straight onto Longfield with this bait and onto the Copse Lake too up at Yateley, where he and I both caught a fish in a short period of time. We didn't go back and fish there anymore, as we actually had our tackle stolen when we were up the pub, so that put an end to us going back on there again. But he was very successful at Longfield; he went on in the first week and caught Jack, the big one, following it up with Big Scale, an amazing fish, which I only ever saw caught once in all the years that we were there.

Some of the fish in Longfield didn't get caught at all while we were there – most of the big commons in there weren't caught. It was the mirrors that were caught. Again I'm not going to go into all the individual captures of all the fish that I had out of there; it's been well documented in my other books, but I was particularly successful on there in the winter when single hookbait fishing was the way to do it. I'd got a particularly good pop-up, which I mentioned earlier in this piece, the Legend, and I went on there with that for the winter and managed to catch about five fish. Floater fishing was my other successful method on there, and most of the ones that I missed out on, I caught off the top during the following summer. I never actually caught Jack; it was one of those bogey fish again, but you can't expect to catch everything, especially when you're fishing with a group of other guys. Steve Alcott was on there with us all the time, and Phil Harper and Dave

Whibley. Ian Guy more or less packed up fishing after the Savay incident, although he came down to Longfield on a few occasions, and I think caught one fish. I believe he had Shoulders, but that was about it, and he didn't fish a lot after that.

Now certainly Fox Pool was one of the most enjoyable places I ever fished, and had it not have been for the lake having to be drained and the fish taken away, I probably would have fished on there for quite a few more years. It certainly had something about it, but for one reason or another, Leisure Sport decided to remove the fish from Longfield and to start a new fishery, a lake called Horton, where they had built a lodge and they had a lovely lake ready to put the fish into. This was going to be the figurehead water for the new company, CEMEX Angling. So very sadly I saw the fish taken away one by one. I went down on numerous occasions to see how the lake was faring, and it was drained down so that the only remaining bit of water was in the top right hand corner of the deepest area of the lake. The structures of gravel on the lakebed were mindblowing and I took pictures of them. Some of the bars were extraordinary columns of gravel appearing in peculiar places all over the lakebed, truly a mega-hard venue because of the weed and just these small areas to hit.

It was a very sad day indeed when I saw Jack taken from the lake. I followed him in the back of the truck down to Horton, and watched about six people have their photographs taken with him before he was put into Horton, which I thought was bizarre. Those incredibly difficult fish to catch threw all caution to the wind over the next few years, and they became the easiest fish in Britain, and anglers caught them in huge numbers. Fish like the Lady, which would make only one appearance at Longfield in a season made ten appearances in the first few months down at Horton. To us of course it threw all their credibility out of the window, but there were a number of anglers fishing for them who had gone on there for some easy pickings and ended up making quite a good reputation for themselves out of catching these fish. You know; people reading the angling papers seeing that Jack had been caught at 45-50lb or whatever out of Horton by this particular angler, are going to think, oh well, what a great angler he must be as we know how difficult that fish is to catch. But what they don't realise is that a change of venue and being totally disorientated in a new lake, those fish became suckers, very easy to catch, and it wasn't long before the majority of them were dead, but there were plenty of other stock fish put in there.

Sitting here doing the piece now in 2011, I believe they're all dead. The last two to go were Shoulders and the Parrot, two tremendous history fish that were moved from water to water over the years. They were both in waters prior to going into Fox Pool, and both made the journey from Fox Pool to Horton safely and became the anglers' favourite fish. I think both those fish, especially Shoulders, became the ones to catch out of Horton. I class myself as very fortunate to have caught it out of Longfield on one of my favourite methods, floater fishing, at a time when carp fishing was in its golden age, when it wasn't all about money and publicity and promoting the latest this or that. It seemed like we just went fishing for pleasure, and that the summers lasted forever. Golden days indeed.

During this time I wrote my first two books, Tiger Bay and Fox Pool. I had several letters of congratulations following their publication and have selected a couple here for you to read. One from Keith Sykes and one from Colin Claydon.

Nod with Jack.

A Letter from Keith Sykes

28th November 1988
R Maylin esq
Dear Rob,
I hope my pen finds both you and all your family well and enjoying the great English weather prevailing upon us currently. I have just finished the autumn/winter newsletter for the Longfield Drinking Team along with completing Tiger Bay for the third time since its publication – and thoroughly enjoyable if I may say so! I always read a book at least three or four times before making a final appraisal; the third time is invariably for content and cataloguing. Tiger Bay has caused a few headaches on the disc, I only had Smithie on file, not his false gnashers, but that has now been taken care of!

I hope you had no objection to my phoning the other evening; it was a genuine desire to know you were well and kicking. Similarly to my writing – if nothing else you may feel the paper to be more applicable to "the Barn"! Apart from your health there were one or two points that I wished to discuss, if you feel so fit as to do so, at your convenience I might add. I had considered mentioning one or two areas when I last saw you at Longfield, but was hesitant on a number of counts, as principally you were angling and the last thing on your mind would be heavy conversation (for want of a better word). There is always a time and place for theoretical chit-chat, and to most anglers it doesn't happen to be when they are contemplating Longfield leviathans. To me it can be at any time or place, but then, as Del tells me, I'm a genetic freak! Before going any further I should like to thank you for your extraordinary hospitality at Longfield; it was warmly and deeply appreciated, the next time it must be on me – do you like Grouse (plucked, distilled and bottled)?

If I wander with my pen I apologise for it is the way my brain works, or doesn't, as the case may be, or perhaps I'm slowly becoming senile… Yes, that must be the answer; it's taken all this time to realise that. Anyway down to my little bits of chatter… In your book you discuss an apparent variation of activity when employing an emulsifying reagent in conjunction with the oils (meat and salmon). The whys and wherefores of emulsifying attractors is, I think, far more complex than even I might have first considered. Let me explain… Apart from carp fishing I've spent many years, too many I suspect, in search of eels. I used to fish with Bob Jones and Pete Climo a lot, both exceptional all-round anglers, with like minds. Big eels are in my humble opinion, by far the most difficult fish to capture consistently for a number of reasons, which are irrelevant here. However, my interest in eels both as an angler and a scientist led me into endeavouring to exploit their highly sensitive olfactory system (about 20 times more acute than that of the carp).

In the mid to late 60s we used either fish or worms for the bulk of our eel angling, and naivety with bait was on a similar parallel to carp angling at the time. We were injecting our baits with various fish and animal oils – horrible sticky aromas. Due to the nature of an oil I thought that if the product was water soluble the level of attraction would be greatly enhanced, and so it turned out, both in field and tank situations. The surfactant (emulsifying agent) I used initially was sodium lauryl sulphate (used widely in the soap manufacturing industry. I used it because a) it is an extremely good oil/water surfactant, b) it's readily available, and c) it cost me nothing! Its drawback is that it is carcinogenic to the respiratory system, which answers a few headaches of a personal nature that arose later in my life.

Back to emulsified oils in use; we found that whilst the number of takes we had only increased minimally (<2% per annum), the hours we waited for takes decreased, which was advantageous when fishing short sessions. I think what has arisen today in terms of emulsifying oil attractors is that attractor to emulsifier compatibility isn't always perfect (the chemical configuration of the attractor is changed, leading to a reduced 'attraction') and that the oil isn't properly emulsified. From the description of your emulsified baits I would say that you were not achieving total emulsification. The reason that leads me to say this is that a totally emulsified oil would not rise and settle on the surface. Whilst I might be teaching grandma to suck eggs, emulsification is attaching a surfactant to the oil droplet, creating a 'tail', which will take the oil into the water media. Simply, if it is turning the hydrophobic oil into a hydrophyllic oil (water loving), a fully emulsified oil will cloud in water, with no oil droplets appearing at all. If partial emulsification is achieved then the result being sought could be to the detriment of what you were, or are, seeking to achieve. What I think happened is that you succeeded in releasing the oil from the bait, but instead of allowing it to linger around the bait it has risen, reducing the attractive properties.

I am a great believer in natural oils, having used them for more years than I care to recall. They appear to work better than synthetics on slow waters because I'm sure the release is so much slower that attraction is better on a long-term basis, particularly if the fish don't happen to be in residence. However, on Bradleys and Hills I've used the oils to good effect using a combination of straight and emulsified oils. My reasoning behind this principle is to leave a mix of baits that will retain their flavour longer, but at the same time to increase attraction during the period I'm fishing. It has certainly worked well for us in past winters on Bradleys (which is 136 acres). Funny thing; that is the only water where I've had to use seed in the winter to hold the fish. I just couldn't produce enough boiled baits to hold them in the swim – great – a bit like your time at Springwood, and I'm still waiting for the Bradley's forty (which might be two now). Incidentally, for your information the best surfactant available for emulsifying fish, animal and natural oils is Microbiological's TEXAFOR. It is extremely compatible, slightly sweet and very powerful so not much is required.

Whilst on the subject of oils, if you can lay your hands on any, strawberry oil is out of this world, but it is not only difficult to obtain, but extortionate in price at £250 per litre. I was interested to see you had used green mussel lipid extract – was that in a liquid form or powder form? A very complex additive that carp like a lot, I'm surprised that more people haven't cottoned onto it, but most anglers wear blinkers, don't they?

Sorry, I do seem to have gone on – definitely a barn job, but what's worse is that more is to come, if you'll beg my pardon. You get a cigar, put the stereo on while I pour a large glass of the plucked distilled stuff. Are you sitting comfortably on your carp bed? Then I'll begin… There were a lot of other areas within your book that I would like to mention, small points or queries, but they can wait – not a conflict of opinion, just points of interest. I thought your inclusion of some of, or part of, your recipes was good. The chapter on baits was in my opinion one of the best ever written, but I feel you didn't do yourself total justice there. I don't know you well old chap, but astute you are and intelligent to boot. The piece on baits was very illustrative of your views to some extent, but I feel you could have put your reasoning behind your own bait ideals over.

Your book portrays your relationship with bait as being simple baits, but in total reality that of course is not true. You put much into the bait you use – not only its compilation but its appliance, and I liked the latter in particular. People today think a pound of bait a day will make all the carp in the world roll into their awaiting nets. I am a great believer in prebaiting and continuous baiting, circumstance permitting. My first real relationship with a good bait and prebaiting began in 1973 on a 12-acre water near my home (15 minutes). Because of its size (small in comparison to the vast majority of my local waters) prebaiting the whole lake would be feasible, if not arduous and expensive. I was doing research work at the time, which allowed access to very high quality ingredients, but my income was a mere few thousand a year! The bait I used was hydrolysed casein, and hydrolysed calcium caseinate with one or two other bits and pieces and an amino acid attractor with a taste additive. The bait was used in paste form coloured with fuller's earth if my memory serves me correctly. We baited it (Lin, Jamie and myself) for five months, eventually concentrating the bulk in a handful of swims that appeared favourable.

I should point out we had caught fish prior to 73 from here but consistency appeared to be a headache, which I put down to the richness of the water, as rather like Staines it is extremely rich in aquatic vegetation. Whilst the water contains numerous bars and silt pockets, which would be covered in elodea and potamogeton during the height of the summer. Not that it really mattered, as in 15 years of fishing the water seriously I caught a mere handful of carp on the bars. Many other anglers failed on the water because of this; they would only fish in the clear spots, which were inevitably on bars of hard gravel.

The baiting resulted in us catching all but two of the fish in the lake. Ironically one turned out to be a mug of 21-24lbs and the biggest fish, which was estimated to be around 40lb (that was a judgement based on fish we caught). I'm not sure why we never had the mug, as it took floaters and anything else available, but it just didn't come our way – daft isn't it? One bloke caught it six or seven times during the course of two seasons. The big fish has to the best of my knowledge never been caught, and I haven't seen it for two seasons now. Perhaps it has gone to the big pond in the sky or just done a disappearing act – they do don't they? We all caught a lot of big carp, but I'm sure much of it was down to a baiting situation, as no one else got a look in. In fact I've not bettered my best fish from there, caught twice at 38lb 12oz in two successive seasons. We used an awful lot of bait in retrospect, but it went on without change for four years, before changing only a handful of the ingredients. I think that once a food is successfully established, captures can be startling, and this is another reason why proprietary readymades, nuts etc have been so successful – everyone using them is baiting up for everyone else.

Staines had a good run on tigers, and whilst I appreciate tigers are (on the whole) an exceptional nut bait, I'm sure the baiting situation, which resulted in so many people using them, had a large role to play in their success. There is the added bonus that carp help bait every nook and cranny with seed/particles in particular. So that rather conveniently leads me onto 'Longfield carp' and 'boilies'. I'm going to the pub now for a 'swift nick' of heavy Guinness and the other stuff. I'll be back soon; you might join me... Second thoughts you might need a stiff drink to prevent boredom from setting in! Go play with the Optonics.

I had a quick word with Steve Alcott down the road; he blanked and seemed keen as mustard to be back on Longfield next weekend. He asked if I had gone to Tim's chat show at Lechlade on Saturday – by all accounts half of Savay were going down. I didn't, but rather spent some time catching carp, although in retrospect I should have gone along to hear what he had to say for himself. I had a rather irritable letter from him last week running down the lads on L.D.T., informing me (for the second time) that I should know better. Obviously he's got it in for everyone down there – strange... What's the difference between being drunk at Redmire and drunk at Longfield? You've obviously got to be Tim to do it! Enough of that anyway – I'm fed up with all the stupid, perverted gossip that seems to emanate from Sheffield. Carp angling is a strange business; I was salmon fishing in Scotland back in September, and during the course of the morning my ghillie filled my cup to overflowing with the 'real golden nectar'. We had lunch at the local hotel and then back to wrestle with a 13½ft double handed salmon rod – it's the done thing, and no one gets banned. Yes, I think I might have preferred to do more of that this season than worrying about making some stupid error at Longfield, such as having a visit to the barn for 30 minutes and 0.5 second. Enough, and back to the inky waters of the little pool, which has led to many a man leaning and eventually falling over.

I was interested to learn of your comment to 'John Allen Slug' about the bait and carp not eating it. Obviously John wanted to know my views, which led to a lengthy conversation over the phone, by which time we both had circulation problems in both ears and lockjaw!

I take it that your comment has been based on the number of fish caught both this season and in past seasons on boiled baits? I think it is convenient for us to assume that the baits are not being eaten on the basis of a few carp being caught in comparison to the number of rods fished during the season, but is this an oversimplification. To cite an example of bait awareness on the water, I think one might have to consider all types of baits rather than singling out boiled baits. Last season Ian introduced 25kg of tigers into the 'Pier Swim' fishing nuts on the hook. This was during a season when carp were still being caught on tigers, but their overall effect was slowing down in comparison to the two seasons prior to this, which is I suspect understandable considering the number of fish having fallen to them.

Anyway, back to Ian that particular week; he had put in that amount of bait over two days (1½ precisely), and at the end of the third day it hadn't been touched, although carp had been seen to enter the swim. On the fourth day it had all gone, leaving only his hookbaits untouched (?). Two seasons ago I had made up my mind to plough in as much bait as I could. It's a 1½ hour drive, which meant five hours in all (there, putting it in and returning). Due to business and college commitments time is always at a premium, and May/June is the yearly nightmare, so trips down to the water often meant arriving at dusk. I managed only a handful of visits, but on days when I managed to be there for more than a few hours they ate the lot, but then they were also eating anything and everything else they came across. No hard and fast conclusions could be made from such observations.

My first week on the pool that particular year wasn't until July (term ended last week of June, so exams marked etc). I always had July to October free (not bad I suppose). My intention was to get in as much as I could, hoping that they'd have it and one (or two!) make a fatal mistake. The first day saw me trickle in 5lb of boiled baits (in the Secret Swim), and that night I didn't get to the pub until 10-ish, as I just sat in wonder watching huge lumps rolling in and crashing over the baits (no rods had been cast out incidentally). I was extremely confident that it was going to happen, and in fact if it hadn't been for 'Brewer's Yeast' coming to collect me from the pub, I would have been content to just have just sat there. I returned from the pub rather more sober than usual, and Steve, Del and I sat sipping iced Grouse watching and listening to the fish crash out over the patch. Dilemma had set in – should I cast out? In the end we sat there until the first grey fingers of a new day dawned, by which time only the odd fish had rolled over the patch. Either they had stopped or were feeding now, but still I refused to cast out. I used the duck to put out another five mixes, this method only causing minimal disturbance and allowing pinpoint accuracy with baiting – essential at the pool (I feel). That night the water rocked again and I went up the pub at 7pm, not being able to stand the tension, and quietly I was hoping my plan was working.

I arrived back at the lake in the early hours having consumed a very large helping of Indian, and the barn saw me earlier than usual that day. I put in another three mixes at tea time before cooking and winding my merry way to the Feathers – tonight I planned to chuck some hooks at 'em. I left the pub early, as I needed to be in full control of my body (if that is ever possible). The duck chugged out and dropped the first hookbait out with about 50 or so freebies. The second rod went out with no hiccups. I was happy, and so out came the second bottle of the week. I was enjoying the solitude, but thought it best to be of a similar vein to the rest of the lads when they returned from the pub, not that I needed to worry – it was like flies around the jam pot, only it was my Grouse bottle that night. I enjoyed it; the element of sharing something personal with one's peers, and great tales were told that night before adjourning to the carp houses.

I was up to see another dawn, and was a little disappointed not to have received a banked carp during the night, as they were still there. Just at the turn of 5am I was away; my heart raced, and soon I had an angry leviathan shaking its head. After removing two weedbeds, the Spiroflex was doing its job, and then it happened – the fish rolled under the attached weedbed, the tip shot up and then twanged back into its original hooped position (where was the Grouse bottle?). It had to be a heave-ho situation, and slowly the mass of weed and fish came closer, inch-by-inch, but then it was gone! I turned to the tree, hit it with my head, and the resulting effect was ideal – I knocked myself out. A while later I dragged the mess in, and the bloody hook had gone, a size 8 salmon hook, the first to let me down. To say I was gutted would have been an understatement – I got drunk at 12.00 that day, but the carp stayed for another day. I didn't fish that day or night; I was incapable and too gutted, but I did, with someone's help, put some more bait out. I had two more chances two days later; one didn't develop, and the other I lost in a weedbed. I packed up one day earlier than planned and came home. I had done everything right, but my luck just hadn't held out – something that happened on a few occasions that season.

My bait had been a HNV type, employing enzymes, aminos and an oil, not commercially available, which has worked well. I'm sorry to have exasperated the point, but I had always felt that perhaps not enough bait was going in. I accepted that examination would continue, and that sometimes you can defeat the object of getting pick-ups with too much grub out there. However, if a thirty and a couple of its smaller brothers decided they wanted it, a mix was hardly going to satisfy the need. I had another similar situation occur in late August (the morning of the famous Summer LDT carp party – what a day). I think that was the morning when John found a taste for the Famous Grouse, and whilst we sat there from 5 till 11.30 my lines didn't stop moving. None of us really knew whether I should hit them or leave it until they flew. As it happened they never flew; I had a chew-off and one crushed hook. At what point during the line lifting it happened I couldn't tell you, but I did have a lot of fish in front of me, rolling and bubbling. We all got very drunk that day, but I thought the bait was working, and was it down to quality or quantity or both? I had about ten mixes out in 48 hours before lift off, and only one other fish was taken that weekend (a 22lb common off the top in the Pier), or for that matter over three weeks.

For the record John, Steve and I had a litre of Grouse for breakfast/brunch, then nine of us descended upon the Percy at lunch. I drank Guinness; the rest 1644, a round each. Into the off licence at Staines, 48 cans of Holsten/Grolsch, two litres of Scotch and then back to the Percy at 6pm. In between we all went for a swim to check the spots and have a drink with Big Scale. I taped the afternoon's conversation, which surprisingly enough is very legible and interesting. The rest of the week saw little angling done and loads of money spent – what a party, seven days long! Sorry, I'm digressing. Steve checked my baits as I packed up; he loves swimming and should have been a big leather carp – not one left!

I hope the situations I've mentioned illustrate the two extremes, but what conclusions can be drawn from this? Well the problem is that a water can vary tremendously from season to season, influenced by numerous factors. Let me ask you a simple question: why do the carp in Longfield need to eat our baits, either boiled/paste baits or particles (to use a generalisation for the latter)? They don't... Or do they? Confusing, am I not? I think it is important that we classify the type of water Longfield is; a scientific classification. It has to be classified as such; it's not good enough to just say Longfield is a rich water, because clearly that is an assumption made due to the dense aquatic vegetation, but Longfield isn't as rich as one might at first suspect. Forgive me for introducing a few words of a technical nature, but this I hope might explain things a little better. Lakes can be categorised simply into two basic types: EUTROPHIC AND OLIGOTROPHIC. A eutrophic lake is one in which the hypolimnion (that is the lower layer of cold water) becomes depleted of oxygen during the summer, and oligotrophic in which it does not. The oxygen in the hypolimnion is used up by the decay of organic matter, which falls from the upper layer (epilimnion). A eutrophic lake is therefore a rich lake. There are other classifications, but for our interest these are the two classifications we need to know; that is, to realise what makes things tick down there. Eutrophic lakes are shallow, but that is relative – Longfield is shallow in comparison to the oligotrophic lakes of the Lake District (for example) (14-18ft in comparison to over 100ft).

We know Longfield has dense, lush aquatic vegetation, which although fluctuating is nevertheless relatively stable. This season it hasn't been so dense as last season, but then many aquatic plants are cyclic in their growing patterns. For instance elodea tends to have a ten-year cycle; the tenth season tends to be very poor, at times almost non-existent, and it may well be that this has been the tenth year for elodea at Longfield. I don't know, although I am sure Ian (The Captain) would. Longfield has vast areas of detritus, made up predominantly from aquatic vegetation and leaves falling from the tree-lined bank. There are one or two areas where this detritus has never been fully degraded – off the trees is a classical example, and there is one area that is foul. Now I appreciate carp will stick their heads into virtually everything, but I believe there are areas where they prefer to frequent only through necessity or when the right conditions prevail – certainly this appears to be the case within the Tree swim. So let us try to build up a picture of what is probably happening at Longfield, which gives rise to low numbers of fish being captured.

I haven't bothered to put in the aquatic vegetation, as its profusion would virtually cover the rough side view of the lake! We therefore have two definable areas: an area

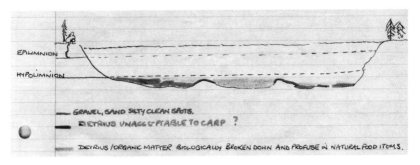

EPILIMNION

HYPOLIMNION

GRAVEL, SAND SILTY CLEAN SPOTS.

DETRIUS UNACCEPTABLE TO CARP ?

DETRIUS /ORGANIC MATTER BIOLOGICALLY BROKEN DOWN AND PROFUSE IN NATURAL FOOD ITEMS.

rich in oxygen and an area that is relatively devoid (obviously not totally but significantly) due to large amounts of organic matter building up. The lower part of the lake will also be colder, and it is very noticeable at Longfield that at about 9.30 Longfield carp begin to move into the upper reaches of the epilimnion (it's warmer). Are they however moving into this zone purely because of warmth? I think not, but also because the area will be oxygen enriched, and therefore likely to be the richest part of the lake in terms of free swimming/crawling food items. There are three prerequisites for organic matter decay to take place: i) oxygen supply (silt that stinks horribly isn't fully decayed) ii) the correct pH (acidic) and iii) an ample population of aerobic bacteria which obviously depend on a good supply of DO2 (dissolved oxygen). Oh yes, I should have also said the temperature has to be correct for bacterial degradation of plant material (silly boy, Sykes). This is true of terrestrial organic matter decay as well as aquatic. So with these optimum requirements we would be looking at peak decay (in true terms) during the spring/summer months, with reduced or no activity during the winter. Graphically this may be illustrated thus:

32° is hypothetical. It is highly unlikely it would ever be as low as this on the bottom. The bloody fish would all be dead.

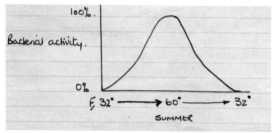

Text for drawing: 32° is hypothetical. It is highly unlikely it would ever be as low as this on the bottom – the bloody fish would all be dead!

So a pattern begins to emerge: in the summer the DO2 level is going to be at its lowest during higher temperatures because of elevated bacterial activity. This might be so stressful that large areas of the lake would be too uncomfortable for a fish to survive in. Come the autumn/winter period, whilst degradation may be minimal, we would be seeing the next deposit of leaves and aquatic vegetation being laid down. This can amount to a vast quantity of organic matter build up, which begins to reduce the pH to an acidic level, again perhaps not acceptable to feeding carp. Naturally, you will be thinking if this is the cause there would be no carp ever captured off the bottom. Well indeed you might ask! Obviously there will be areas where the organic matter is low or where degradation is complete and there are ideal feeding areas for the fish. However, I would surmise that there are long periods when the carp do not go near the bottom, this statement applying to both the summer and winter period. Anglers have for a long time written off waters for winter fishing because there is such a comparable difference in catch rates. Accepting everything being equal, then I think there are a lot of waters that don't fish well simply because of the state of the bottom; I don't think it's simply down to water temperatures decreasing.

In terms of the best food supplies I would imagine that in Longfield these are restricted principally to areas – well off bottom in well oxygenated water, which is an also the warmest and areas of silt/detritus where total degradation has taken place. So there will be large areas of the lakebed where carp may never feed or only feed at certain times, and it could be when the latter occurs that fish are caught. If this is the case then there will be vast amounts of bait that are never eaten by anything, save perhaps waterfowl. In reality it is difficult to ascertain just how much bait is taken by waterfowl (and eels I ought to add), but I think it is more than we give credit for. One would also imagine that more bait would appear on the surface. Well, in the case of particles I think you'll just achieve a mass of rotting waste, and to some extent with boiled baits. One also has to consider how much bait never reaches the surface through being caught up in the matrix of vegetation. All these factors could result in few baits ever been seen on the surface, although I have found odd smelly concoctions in the margins that even coots found too obnoxious to consume!

Naturally I don't believe that that the cause for so few carp being caught is down totally to the biological nature of the lake, although I am now convinced it has a very large bearing on the feeding patterns. Let me finish this by pointing out the other influencing factors as I see them, that is, accepting there are times when a lot of bait will be consumed.

To start with Longfield carp don't need to rely upon any form bait; the lake may be at its peak of productivity (I say this because of certain carp rarely fluctuating in weight, even accepting their ages), but the total biomass must be enormous and certainly sufficient to keep the residents healthy, and not only the carp either!

I'm sure that much of the time we're not fishing the right areas, and I don't mean just the right area on the bottom, but rather off the bottom. The first carp I ever hooked in Longfield (I had two takes on my first weekend there) was in March on the Bungalow Bank. I was fishing two entirely different setups after discussing things with Steve. He had commented about the beds of leaves and the dead/dying weed matting itself on the bottom. Often this reeked and he wasn't happy about baits fished in such conditions, with justification.

I decided to fish two different zones, as I couldn't find suitable hard, clear spots of any size, convinced they were covered in dying weed. One rig was a straightforward long braided hooklink (2½in) with a neutral buoyancy bait (featherlight) and a 2oz glass bomb. The glass bomb sinks extremely slowly, settling on top of anything. The second rig was something I had adopted from pike fishing live baits, and one with which you might be familiar with. I first saw this being used by Dick Walker on Loch Lomond at Portnellan Bay. Viz:

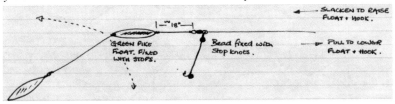

I suppose the way the bait was presented looked totally unnatural, but I cast the lot out into a weedbed, set to fish at about 8ft off the bottom. To be honest I didn't think I'd stand a look in, but every other lead was being thumped to any available clear spot, so I had nothing to lose. I lost a fish on the second night on the suspended boilie – blue cheese and garlic oil on meta-bait in a huge mat of weed on the surface in front of me. In retrospect I should have jumped in, but it was two in the morning and bloody cold. I also had another take the same night but missed the bloody thing. If I remember that was it for the season, although I think Steve or Paul lost one on the same pike rig. Subsequently I've watched those fish going through the beds of weed, down the tunnels created with time, feeding merrily on their way. It was a method that I didn't exploit or develop because it certainly had tangle problems, and distance can be a problem. I have proved it works by catching carp in the winter at Horseshoe Lake in the snags, whilst bottom baits have remained untouched. Looking back I should have persevered with the method at Longfield, but then last year was a year I choose to put aside. Add to this the fact of what percentage of bait never reaches the deck could, along with natural circumstances, lead to further suggestion that the carp's larder is a far cry from the bottom strata of the lake?

It is difficult to totally evaluate the quantity of bait going into a water, although in theory it should be easier on a water the size of Longfield. To this end one would need to consider the following: i) how much bait reaches the bottom, ii) how much is eaten by the carp (if any), iii) how much bait is eaten by other species; tench, bream etc, iv) how much is never consumed by anything, and v) how much is removed either on the bottom or the surface by waterfowl. Such answers are only theoretically predictable.

Finally then, if one assumes that the carp do eat boiled baits, which obviously they do at times, if not possibly all the time, why aren't more carp caught? Is it simply down to the years of pressure and the intensity of such that lead the carp to be ultra-aware, and mistakes resulting in banked fish? For instance when John caught the forty in the winter (well late December, but it was unusually mild) there was another fresh hook mark in the lunker's mouth. I examined the fish thoroughly and that fish had four hooks embedded in its mouth. Two were healed (John off the top and Bernie off the bottom in the summer), and the freshest was John's in the winter, but there was another beginning to heal. The only fish I know of lost in between Bernie's capture and John's capture was in the November by Del in the Little Noddy. Did he lose that fish, or had that fish got rid of the hook without notifying the silly sod on the bank? We will never know, but it makes you think. In the winter last year we all had a lot of single bleeps – fish or just settlement? The questions are endless, but then that is surely the fascination of carp angling, isn't it?

Earlier I mentioned weed tunnels. We all try to find clear spots, the smaller the better, but do the carp feed regularly on such spots? Perhaps not. Is a bait presented around food rich silt presented in the correct area, particularly as it is likely the freebies eventually sink into (to some level) the silt? I've watched my two big carp feeding in the tank; they've been hooked (for evaluation) numerous times, and are beginning to get old. I'm still amazed that we actually hook carp at times; we assume too much, and anthromorphosise to an even greater extent. When is a 3oz lead not 3oz? When it's in water.

I'll go, because no doubt you have better things in life to do than read my rattling, prattling pen scribble. I've mentioned much, but in reality only scraped the surface. A carp is a carp after all, but as you rightly say in your book, why does a flavour suddenly blow? If all the carp resident had been hooked then we could explain it away logically, but when 25-50% never get hooked (?) how do they know? I remember talking to Rod about this back in 80/81 – inter-specific communication, pheromones, I don't know. I've got my theories, but then as they say that is another story, or ten pages of A4 as the case may be! One thing I had noticed is that I've experienced greater activity on an attractor that is blowing out after its been in the water for 48 hours or more. Is it because the attractor has virtually dissipated leaving an inherently attractive food source? Maybe.

So as I said I'll go. I hope I've not caused you to have a migraine, but have perhaps opened up something for you to consider in between building trucks on computers. I wish you continued success and happiness.

Keep your face to the sun and your shadow will always follow!

Good luck and kindest regards.

Keith

Every lake has its own quality, and it is the part of wisdom to know and love as many as you can.

A Letter from Colin Claydon

29.12.90

Dear Rob,

If I was given your book Fox Pool to read by a friend a week or two ago, and took the opportunity of reading it over Christmas. At this early point, I should mention that I fished Longfield and Yeoveney from 1967-71, but stopped fishing after that. However your book has rekindled my enthusiasm.

The following notes may be of interest to you. Before Hall and Co took control of Longfield, the lake was controlled by a local club who only ever match fished it. From time to time the matchmen hooked the odd carp and very occasionally one was landed – usually over 25lbs. These were very big fish for those days (1965-70). At that time I doubt there were more than 15 big fish in there, plus a few commons in the 8-10lb range. However there were three or four very big fish (even then) seen by many good anglers (Hilton, Mintram etc) and we all thought the 'top' was 32lb-plus. Bear in mind that fish that big were very few and far between and we were all careful not to over-exaggerate the size.

The biggest fish I ever saw was in Cable Corner and I put it at 38lb (but in spawn). I hooked this fish twice in this corner on flake but lost it both times on the cables. Len Arbery fished just along from there and asked me to try to remove a sunken tree with a tractor and chain (we failed). This leads me to think he may have lost the big one as well, but Len was never one to give up his secrets!

Your theory on the feeding areas is very interesting, and I would have to agree with you that fish never feed in certain areas. We found that if you found the chub you found the carp. Was this so with you? Having said that, the chub didn't show very often either!

When we were on the lake, carp very rarely showed on the top and never leapt at all. The weed was very thick, often there were only five or six swims and they were only gravel in the margins! One year it was so thick you couldn't get a 2oz lead through it! The tench population was a bloody nuisance, and it was nothing to get four or five fish in a morning, averaging 5lbs.

To say the lake was hard is another understatement. Like yourself, I went 41 nights without a touch and couldn't believe it could be that difficult, but it was obvious that the fish only feed in certain areas, and if those swims were gone, then you were better off going to the pub! The only certain area was the Bungalow Bay, where the old lady feeds the fish by hand!

We tried all we know (remember in those days we were using bread, pastes and 'taitas') and the place drove you mad! We used to go to Yeoveney for light relief – by comparison it was a doddle of a water.

On the second year at Longfield, I thought I'd cracked it. I'd had nothing but tench through the night and decided to put out a crust (to feed the geese!). Having hooked a goose (just to put a bend in the rod you understand!) and missed a couple more, I decided to try something different. Out went another crust on a 6ft link to beat the weed and when it popped up, I wound it back down some 2-3ft from the top. That fooled the geese! Couldn't believe my luck when away it went and I got a common of 1½lb. The next morning it happened again, but I was robbed. The beast went 18lb 14oz but was the ugliest thing I ever caught. It should have gone about 25lb but its body was as thin as a bream! I could only imagine it was dying, as I've never seen a carp so emaciated.

That was it that year, but the following year I did manage another proper fish of 26lb 10oz on the same method. I don't think anybody else was using the sunken crust because they didn't believe me! I fished it for three years on and off and got nine twenties with the best over 26lb but didn't fish it after 1971. This is where the interest in your book ties in with the fish you were catching. Checking the photos your fish were definitely the fish we had in the 67-71 period, but what interests me is that there was a common in Yeoveney that I saw twice (when they were spawning) and it was BIG. One night at Yeoveney in a gale I had the bugger, only to lose it at the net through the hook failing and I'm certain to this day it was over 30lb then, so what happened to it? Did it get netted out and moved to Longfield with the others? Did they miss it? Did it die? Did it go somewhere else?

I can assure you this fish existed; several people saw it and all agreed it was 10lbs heavier than the mirrors we were catching, but it's not mentioned in your book. This

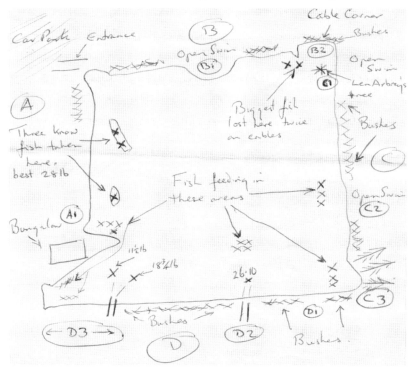

is what's bugging me. What happened to that fish, or did it go into Longfield never to be seen or caught?

Believe me it was a hell of a fish for that period. I saw Pete Bradely's 30 from Redmire and I would say it was slightly bigger than that. Can you throw any light on this?

The map is very crude but it shows where we caught or saw fish, which will, I think, prove your theory of non-feeding areas:-

Hope you can make some sense of this. The three fish from bank A (Noddie Bank in your book?) were taken when I wasn't there, but I know they are correct. Area (A1) often had two or three large mirrors in the tanks in the corner but to my knowledge nobody got a look in here.

Swim (B1) doesn't look any different in your book except that you got fish from it and we couldn't! When we were there it was blocked solid with weed. (B2) This was the corner with the sunken coils of cable. After losing the big fish for the second time I gave up here, convinced you'd never get the fish out. It was also very heavily weeded.

(C1) Len always fished here and I think had some success despite the sunken tree.

(C2) Loads of tench. Carp seem to feed but were never caught.

(C3) Often had the most carp in this corner. I personally counted 11 one day including the big one, but I never got a touch. The sight of a crust here spooked them.

(D1) Full of tench and the odd bream.

(D2) I twice saw fish here and got one of them.

(D3) the Bay swim – fish always here – especially when the old lady feeds the geese. I got two here in 24 hours.

Well I hope this has interested you in some way. As I said earlier it was your book that prompted me to write it down on paper. It's a pity the lake has gone for it had a certain 'aura' even when I fished it.

It drove you mad, but you kept going back! A real bastard water!

Thanks for the info in the book – it is one of the best I've read. Maybe I'll start again if I can ever fangle out these modern rigs!

Yours,

C Claydon

Chapter 5
Famous Five Forever — Lifelong Friends

"Being the sort of anglers we are, we couldn't go fishing without going to the pub or a nightclub."

So Savay Lake was now a distant memory and there was little chance of ever getting back over there and fishing, and the Copse Lake didn't really work out for us, with both Dave Whibley and I having all our tackle stolen one night on there while we were at the pub. Being the sort of anglers we are, we couldn't go fishing without going to the pub or a nightclub or something at night. Fishing was done in the daytime and the fun was at night, and if we couldn't have fun at night worrying about our tackle, we certainly weren't going to fish there.

We thought we'd found a new home with Longfield; it was an amazing water and we met some great guys there as well. Perhaps before I dismiss Fox Pool and move onto Johnsons, I should tell you about some of the funny things that went on there. Obviously I've written a lot about the fishing in my other books, so I won't go too much into that; those stories are there if you want to read them any time, and there seems little point really going over our fishing adventures, but some of our night time adventures were never written about, and maybe this is the place to tell you about those.

First of all the friends we met there who have become lifelong friends. I suppose really Johnny Allen and Colin Martin were the first two. I actually met John over on the North Lake at Yateley and he took me over to Longfield one day after our weekend's fishing. I did do one or two odd weekends on the North Lake at this time after Bazil, one or two sort of hit-and-miss weekends a year, and not really worth mentioning here, as my campaign didn't really start there until the early 90s. There was John Holt too, who was one of the first guys we met when we went over to Longfield. He was very open about his captures, and he brought his photograph album along one night up to the Percy (The Perseverance pub) in between Fox Pool and Wraysbury. It was the pub that the Wraysbury guys used; it wasn't the pub that we used. There was another pub closer to the lake that the Longfield guys used, The Feathers, and oh boy, did we have some fun in there. I'll get to that in a moment.

Peter Jones and his friend Dave from Brighton were two other great guys we met on there, and Steve Briggs too. Terry Dempsey, Jeff Bowers... When I think about it there were lots and lots of really good guys, some of whom stayed with us on our travels after Fox Pool was netted and closed down. As we moved on from water to water a few of these guys came with us, in particular of course Steve Briggs, Pete and Dave who told us about Johnsons where we ended up going after there.

But anyway, back to these nights at The Feathers. Wow, where do I start? We left Savay as very angry men; we felt as though we'd been hard done by.

I say we; it was mainly Steve and I, to be honest. Phil Harper, he was just a fanny magnet; he couldn't go anywhere without attracting the opposite sex. When I think about it, there were very few nights that we went out where he didn't actually pull someone and end up bringing her back to the lake and we were so jealous of him. He was a handsome chap, and he's living in the Philippines now so I understand with about three wives and living like a king out there – good old Pippy.

Ian Guy, or 'Trotter', Steve's companion from the Black Country, was quite an angry little guy too and ended up getting into all sorts of scrapes. He had Steve and I in stitches some nights when we ventured off to The Galleon, and I'll tell you about that in a moment. It was the start of the Acid House era so it was a wild time. Dave Whibley was far too quiet to get involved in any of this shenanigans but more than happy to come along for the ride, and Martin Locke too, quiet but enjoying all the fun.

We all made sure that when we went for a weekend's fishing we had plenty of going out clothes with us, which involved at least three ironed shirts, trousers in case we wanted to go to a nightclub, and shoes, as most of the nightclubs of that era didn't let you in with jeans and trainers. We took plenty of aftershave and shaving equipment, and oh God, when I think back to Phil Harper fishing in the North Bay on the North Lake… Come five o'clock in the evening, he'd wade out into the North Bay to shave, and all this white fluffy shaving foam would be floating out across to Bazil's Bush. How we actually caught anything I'll never know, but the nightclubbing and going out was more important than the fishing, or at least as important as the fishing.

We really did enjoy ourselves, and wherever we went, we started off at The Feathers. What would normally happen was, about seven o'clock we went down to The Feathers, all togged up, laughing and joking and full of anticipation at what the night would bring. Going down to The Feathers pub, which was a few hundred yards down the road, involved going past about thirty unfortunate houses, which, during the couple of years we were there, had to put up with all sorts of noise from us returning to the lake when the pubs kicked out. I do apologise; we were angry young men…

So we would make our way down to The Feathers and then decide what we would do later on, which might involve a curry or a pub-crawl in Staines. I remember going to Staines one night with a guy called Mad Mick from Kent. We bought some chips on the way home, and for some reason Mick had decided he wanted to set fire to the chip papers. He was getting further and further behind Steve, me and another couple of guys. We were walking back from Staines, and it was a good hour and a half's walk back to the lake

– we'd missed any chance of a taxi or anything. He began lighting all these bits of paper, and by the time we got back to the lake and had a cup of tea, there was no sign of Mick. Well unbeknown to us he'd been arrested that night and charged with arson of all things – 'arson of the highway', which I'd never heard of. Apparently the last person to be charged with arson of the highway was in 1806, so, well done Mick anyway. We did laugh when we found out; he spent the night in the nick and came back to the lake in the morning.

So another favourite haunt was The Galleon pub at Chertsey. It was a full-on Acid House night up there on a Friday or a Saturday night, one of the two nights, anyway. It was a good way from Fox Pool; it meant a taxi, or if there were a lot of us, a minibus, but it was crazy times – people were just off their heads over there. Across the bridge was a club, the Chertsey nightclub, where they were very strict about who got in. I remember one particular funny story… There were about probably fifteen of us who had gone up to The Galleon on this particular night, and the pub had an extension; they let you drink through until midnight. We'd booked taxis but they hadn't picked us up; they'd taken us over there and taken the money but they hadn't come to get us. They probably thought, well, that

The Johnson's leather – front cover of Big Carp magazine No. 1.

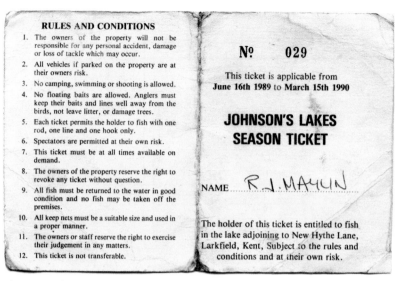

RULES AND CONDITIONS

1. The owners of the property will not be responsible for any personal accident, damage or loss of tackle which may occur.
2. All vehicles if parked on the property are at their owners risk.
3. No camping, swimming or shooting is allowed.
4. No floating baits are allowed. Anglers must keep their baits and lines well away from the birds, not leave litter, or damage trees.
5. Each ticket permits the holder to fish with one rod, one line and one hook only.
6. Spectators are permitted at their own risk.
7. This ticket must be at all times available on demand.
8. The owners of the property reserve the right to revoke any ticket without question.
9. All fish must be returned to the water in good condition and no fish may be taken off the premises.
10. All keep nets must be a suitable size and used in a proper manner.
11. The owners or staff reserve the right to exercise their judgement in any matters.
12. This ticket is not transferable.

N° 029

This ticket is applicable from
June 16th 1989 to March 15th 1990

JOHNSON'S LAKES
SEASON TICKET

NAME   R.J.MAYLN

The holder of this ticket is entitled to fish in the lake adjoining to New Hythe Lane, Larkfield, Kent, Subject to the rules and conditions and at their own risk.

Johnson's Lake ticket 1989. Note rule 5, (1 ticket = 1 rod).

N° 22953 **A**

Southern Water

1989/90

Rod & Line Licence

SECOND ROD ONLY
Licence Duty
£1.50

THIS BOX TO BE ~CKED IF ~ ROD

No. 22953

Southern Water

SALMON AND FRESHWATER FISHERIES ACT 1975, WATER ACT 1973

Licence Duty **£6.00**   **1989/90**
Fishing (Rod & Line) Licence · Trout
(INCLUDING MIGRATORY TROUT, FRESH WATER FISH & EELS)

ANNUAL LICENCE
NOT TRANSFERABLE   Date of Issue 3/6/19 89

Mr Ro9 MAYLIM of 6STH4 Countohs
FLITWICK BEDS.

is hereby licensed to use one rod and line to fish in the area for trout (including migratory trout, freshwater fish and eels). An angler using more than one rod and line at the same time must hold sufficient current fishing (rod and line) licences for all such rods and lines. This licence is valid until 31st March 1990. This licence does not entitle the holder to fish in the relevant close seasons (see Note 3 overleaf).

IT DOES NOT CONFER A RIGHT TO FISH IN ANY WATERS.

GUILDBOURNE HOUSE, CHATSWORTH ROAD, WORTHING, WEST SUSSEX BN11 1LD

THE FRIENDLY FISHERMAN

Signature of Licence Holder   Issued by: Distributor

PLEASE READ THE NOTES ON THE BACK

(This licence must be produced on demand to any water bailiff, con~ ~any other licensee producing his own licence).

Guildbourne House, Chatsworth Road, Worthing, West Sussex BN11 1LD

Southern Water

Name
Address

Southern Water licence 1989, £6!

Geezer Slyme Gripe was really popular in the early Big Carps.

We've all felt like this at a certain moment in out lives!

Who's got who?

lot are just going to be such a handful on the return journey we won't pick them up.

There was Hippy Paul, the guy was six foot four and a complete lunatic, Tony Moore, Jeff Bowers, me – some big guys anyway. We'd got as drunk as we possibly could, and at then 12.30 we were outside The Galleon looking up and down the road for our taxis. So I thought to myself, look, I've got to get away from this lot because there's no way that four taxis will come along to pick us up, which is what we needed. So I decided to scoot off over the bridge, up to the Chertsey nightclub and phone for a taxi from there, so off I went. Well, unbeknown to me, Jeff Bowers had seen me go and followed me a hundred yards or so behind. When I got to the door of the Chertsey club, the doorman took one look at me and said I couldn't come in and I couldn't use the phone, so there was no way I could call a taxi.

Anyway, the club car park was packed; it was a busy night in the club that night. Every little nook and cranny had a car in it and as I looked across the car park, I saw a guy just getting in his car, so I ran across the car park and said, "Hello mate, my taxi's let me down, which way are you going and any chance of a lift?" So he said, "Well, I'm going up the M25." So I said, "If you could drop me off just by junction 13 of the M25, I could walk back to the lake I'm fishing." He said, "You're fishing are you? Oh yeah, of course mate, your taxi let you down, what a shame. Jump in the front because I've got a lot of hat boxes in the back." He had an estate car and the back was filled up with these boxes, which he informed me had got some hats in.

Anyway with that, there was a knock at my window and Jeff Bowers was there. So the guy looked at me and said, "Who's that?" I said, "Oh, it's one of my fishing mates, is it alright if he gets in?" So he said, "Yeah, yeah, go on, let him in. Push those boxes to one side and get him in the back." So I said, "You're in luck Jeff, jump in the back, push those boxes over. They're hats, be careful. He's going to drop us off at junction 13 on the M25." "Oh brilliant," he said. Anyway, with that, we looked across the car park, and who should be coming but the rest of the guys. There was a good dozen of them, all big fellas, and they were heading towards the car. The bloke looked at me, his face went white and he said, "Who are that lot?" I said, "Oh that's the rest of our party." I said, "If I were you I'd get out of here because they're going to want a lift home as well." He absolutely crapped himself, slammed the car into reverse and skidded backwards, bang, straight into a car behind us. He was pinned in and he was going to need about a five-point turn to get the car out of there.

With that, all fifteen of these guys descended on the car, beating on the roof, jumping on the bonnet, and the bloke just absolutely freaked. He slammed it into first gear and whizzed forward, smashing into the car to his left, then backwards again, crash, as he hit the car behind, and then forward again. Well he did his five-point turn, but with every point he hit a car in different directions and then skidded, with a massive great wheel-spin, out of the car park with all the fishing guys chasing, screaming and shouting behind him and beating on the boot. Jeff and I were in absolute hysterics, but the bloke was so pleased to get away. He was saying, "Oh my God, oh my God, they looked like they were going to kill me." I said, "No, no, they wouldn't have killed you, but they were dying for a lift home. You'd have had them in the boot and everywhere if they could have got in here."

Anyway, what a diamond this guy turned out to be; he drove us all the way back to the lake, which involved unlocking the gate and driving down the bumpiest track you have ever driven down in your life. He grounded the bottom of the car at least ten times before he got to the lake, as there were so many potholes in the track. But he dropped us right off at the lake and then set off, probably grateful that he was still alive, but what a laugh. The others all ended up walking back from The Galleon at Chertsey, which must have taken them three or four hours.

As I said there were about thirty houses down the little road between the lake and The Feathers pub, and anything that was moveable normally ended up back at the lake, including things like, 'For Sale' signs. If any of those houses went up for sale you could bet your life that someone would pull the sign out of the ground and end up sticking it in a swim on Fox Pool. I remember one night there were some roadworks along there and they had cones and little waterproof boxes with these flashing amber lights, and all that lot ended up back at the lake. In fact the amber lights ended up being thrown into the Noddy swim and you could see them flashing on the bottom in about 15ft of water. If my memory serves me right, it was Pete Jones who was fishing in there, and when he got back to the lake he called me to his swim and said, "Look at that reflection…" He was looking up in the air for an aircraft or something or other, but of course it wasn't a reflection at all; it was actually these lights flashing on the bottom of the lake.

We were a bit out of control I've got to admit, and I'm not proud of some of the things we got up to. We earned the reputation of being lunatics, which was probably the right description, but we were angry; we were angry at getting thrown out of Savay for not doing anything wrong, and we took it out on everything we came across from that point on. Anyway, with the closing down of Longfield, Johnsons seemed the sensible choice and although Trotter, Ian Guy, slipped away from the Five, the rest of us stuck

Kent carp No. 1 from Johnson's.

The beautiful Bent Tail, Johnson's 1989.

1 ticket, 1 rod = 6 tickets, 6 rods!!

Zen scores first.

The very snaggy Snake Pit.

Some great memories.

Me and Alan Partridge on a day trip to Withy Pool.

together and went up to Kent.

Johnsons was lovely; it was a beautiful lake with beautiful fish and very relaxed rules. Most people used little rubber blow-up dinghies for positioning their bait and baiting up. It was a very weedy lake; quite a lot of the guys on there were tench fishermen. A trip into Maidstone by taxi wasn't too far, and there was a pub at the bottom of the road. We'd go down there and have a couple of beers first, then order ourselves a taxi and then go off on our adventures.

Paul Brooks, Phil Harper, Steve, Dave Whibley, Martin Locke, Steve Briggs, Pete, Dave, a few others, and I certainly opened little Steve Wade's eyes up, who was only a boy at the time. One of our favourite haunts was the Malta Pub, beautiful country pub on the banks of the River Medway, and wow, did we get up to some shenanigans down there... Very often we'd end up jumping in the river at the end of the night, swimming round with our beers, and going home in the taxi soaking wet. We must have been crazy when I think about these things, but one night I remember Phil Harper was up on the roof of the pub at the end of the night. Don't ask me what he was doing up there, mucking around. Well, I ended up there too, and Phil said to me, "Look, I'll show you how to do a rolling jump."

So he jumped from the roof, crouched and did a roll, and sprung up. "There you go, that's how you do a jump and roll; they show you how to do that in the army." I thought I could do that, all 15-16 stone of me, so I jumped, but I landed flat-footed, taking all the weight straight on my knees. There was an almighty crack and I fell to the floor in agony. Luckily I was very, very drunk and didn't really feel much until the morning, having got back to the lake and cast the rods out that night. I woke up and found that both my knees had seized up solid and I couldn't bend my legs. Luckily, my good mates Steve and Phil packed all my tackle up and put it in the car. Steve actually carried me back to the car and put me in. I managed to get home anyway, but it took a couple of months before I could walk properly again. I don't know what I did; I never went to the doctor. I mean my leg has got to fall off before I go to the doctor. I'm not scared of doctors, but I just don't go unless something's really, really wrong, and that didn't warrant it as far as I was concerned. They're still painful now twenty-odd years later, so it just shows you how stupid I was.

Another very stupid thing that I used to do now I think about it was collect pot plants from the local Chinese and Indian restaurants and take them back to the lake. Yes, not the cleverest thing to do; you're probably right, but I had quite a little arboretum underneath the willow trees on the far side of the Railway Lake. I'd collected lemon plants in great big pots from the Chinese restaurant, rubber plants, trailing orchids and goodness knows what. How I ever walked out of the takeaways with those pot plants I don't know, but I did. I'd walk out of the Chinese takeaway and get into the back of the taxi with my Chinese takeaway and a massive great pot plant, about 4ft tall, poking out the window. I had them all nicely arranged under the fronds of these weeping willows on the End Willows swim, and I used to water them and tend to them. I don't know what happened to them when we left there; I didn't take them away with me, but it was a source of much laughter on the lake at the time, I can tell you.

Of course plants were not the only things we brought back to the lake; the most sought after thing to bring back of course was young ladies. Maybe this is not the right place to talk about what went on with some of the guys in the group, but let's just say we were good at catching fish, but we were even better at catching females, and we didn't blank very often.

We went there to catch the Johnsons Leather, which was the fish in the lake. We were told before getting there that it would be around 36-38lb, and there was another fish in there called the Dinosaur, which could be 40lb. Well, the Dinosaur ended up not being in there, and the Leather at the time was around 32-34lb. I mentioned earlier how relaxed the rules were, and you could use as many rods as you had rod licences for, so I think I bought eight rod licences. I don't think that I ever used eight rods, but I certainly used seven on more than one occasion. On one particular occasion when I had seven rods out, I wasn't in my swim as it happens; I was up the bank a way with Steve Briggs trying to catch some snakes. One of the guys was a bit scared of snakes, and if we could catch a few and put them in his bivvy that was always a good plan.

A couple walking round the lake came past Briggsy and me and said, "Whose are all those rods down there?" I thought they were having a go about how many rods I'd got out, so I said, "Well they're mine, what of it?" They said, "Well one of them was absolutely flying when we went by," and so I legged it back to the rods. They weren't far away, but far enough not to hear the buzzer, and that was the Leather. It was on the front cover of the Number 1 Big Carp magazine the following year. I'll tell you how that came about because it's another quite amusing story…

As most of you will know, I was a draughtsman; I did a draughtsman engineering apprenticeship on the drawing board for Vauxhall Motors. When computers came in I got trained up on CADAM and CATIA and was soon headhunted by various other automotive companies to work in their design studios. I worked as a draughtsman for Volvo, Renault on a couple of occasions, General Motors, Aston Martin and British Aerospace on two

Phil's in next.

Farlows – what a laugh...

...but some gorgeous carp.

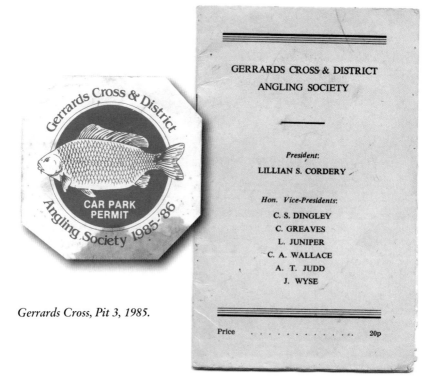

22 Anyone wishing to take a guest to Taplow for angling **must** obtain a guest ticket from their Secretary for a nominated day. You may only take the same guest angling 3 times per season - for further angling they would have to apply for Membership (No charge will be made for guest tickets). Non-angling guests may be present providing they abide by the relevant rules and do not cause any nuisance to other anglers - no large parties.
23 During any match - all fish must be weighed-in in swims and returned promptly to the water.
24 Common and mirror carp must not be kept in keep nets or any other retainer - unless needed for witnessing or photographing - then maximum retention of ¹/₂ hour.
25 Keep nets must be a minimum of 6 ft x 18 ins.
26 All live bait to be caught at Taplow - no live bait to be brought to the Lake.
27 Only this permit valid - no other Club or Recreation Club card is acceptable. Permits must be carried at all times - otherwise angling is forbidden.
28 Cornfields on East and South side of the Lake are out of bounds.
29 No fishing after 12 noon on the previous day of the Annual Challenge Match see Rule 16.
30 No pre-baiting or excessive ground baiting.

TAPLOW LAKE
THIS IS TO CERTIFY THAT THE UNDERSIGNED IS PERMITTED TO FISH TAPLOW LAKE ONLY FOR THE SEASON STATED, AND IS TO ABIDE BY THE RULES STATED ON THIS PERMIT.

Name *RŎ ΠAYLIN*

Club *GERRARDS X* A/S

Season *1986/7*

ISSUED BY ICI PAINTS DIVISION - RECREATION CLUB

Taplow ticket, 1986.

Gerrards Cross, Pit 3, 1985.

GERRARDS CROSS & DISTRICT ANGLING SOCIETY

President:
LILLIAN S. CORDERY

Hon. Vice-Presidents:
C. S. DINGLEY
C. GREAVES
L. JUNIPER
C. A. WALLACE
A. T. JUDD
J. WYSE

Price 20p

Len Gurd, doing what he does best.

Dave with a Pit 3 twenty.

And one for Steve too.

occasions. It was on one of these occasions while working for British Aerospace that my boss at the time, a big, fat guy who liked a beer and obviously got on well with me, asked me if I could manage a project to design a small jet for an Arab customer of theirs. It was mega money for the 80s; I mean I was on about £40K a year, which was a lot of dough. There was no way I was going to turn the work down although I had no idea how to design a jet. My background had been in car design; I'd designed bodies and mechanical parts for the automotive industry since I left school. My six years at university were all to do with automotive engineering, so I had no idea about designing aircraft. Anyway, he was offering me a lot of money; I had about 20 people working for me, and there was no way I was going to turn it down, although I knew I couldn't do it.

So, I set off working on this project for British Aerospace. I had all these guys working for me doing drawings of a jet that the customer had previously owned, which was what this new jet was going to be based around. As I had no idea what I was doing and wanted to at least have a few months there earning some money, I got people drawing, repeating basically the same drawings that we already had. It was back on the drawing board again, as British Aerospace didn't have computer-aided draughting at the time, and this went on from August through to almost Christmas before I got sussed. It was only a week or so before Christmas and a lot of Arab guys and my boss were standing in one of the offices looking at the drawings and looking at me, looking at the drawings and looking at me, and I realised that I'd been sussed.

When I went home that night I said to my first wife, "I've had it; I'm pretty sure they're going to sack me because they must have sussed out that I haven't got a clue what I'm doing and I've only drawn the same old stuff again. I think I'm going to have to hand my notice in and do something different. I'm fed up with this; I'm thinking about doing a carp fishing magazine." She thought I was crazy. I was writing a column in Carpworld at the time and had already written a couple of books, so I knew the ins and outs of publishing and printing. Anyway, I went in to work the next morning, and before my boss had a chance to fire me, I went into his office and said, "Hi Bob, I've got some bad news for you, my old mate. I've got to hand my notice in at Christmas." He turned round to me, and he said, "Oh thank Christ for that. The last thing I wanted to do was fire you, but we were looking at this job yesterday, and you haven't got a clue what you're doing, have you?" I said, "No, let's go for a beer."

We parted on good terms, but that was the end of my drawing life. To be honest, even as a draughtsman in the automotive industry, I never really enjoyed a day's work; I was always thinking about fishing, and the only place I wanted to be was on the bank. So I started the magazine, and although it has had its ups and downs over the years, it was certainly the best thing I ever did. I'm very passionate about Big Carp; I was then in 1991, and I am now 20 years later in 2011. I love the magazine; I love the feedback I get from guys who read it every month who take the time to write in or email or call me and say, "What a mag this month, mate – fantastic, keep up the good work, Rob." You know, those are the sorts of comments that keep you going through the hard times with any small business that you own yourself.

So back to Johnsons... We spent the summer up there, but there were various other waters coming up at the same time, and we found ourselves being torn apart as the Famous Five. We wanted to fish together at all costs, but certain waters materialised over this period of time. The Snake Pit appeared in the Angling Times one week, a lake we'd never heard of, with details of Damian Clark and a pal with a massive 40lb common. A 40lb common was huge for this time, and of course we had to go and investigate that. We ended up meeting with Zen and little Rael Bojko and had some great times with them. They came to Harefield with us, and Broadlands after that, but of course Steve and Phil and I wanted to fish for this 40lb common. It was on Phil's and Zen's doorstep, so they were destined to catch it really, what with it only being ten minutes' down the road from where they lived. It was a good three-hour drive for Steve on a Friday afternoon in the rush hour, and a couple of hours for me too, as I was still working as a draughtsman. Finishing work at 5pm on Friday afternoon and then hitting the traffic on the M25 was not conducive to catching a lot of fish or getting a decent swim. But we had fun up there too; I mean the nightlife once again was excellent. We used to go into Colchester and hit the pubs and the clubs in that area. Phil and I had some great times; we used to go out and pretend we were pilots one night, and then another night we'd be doctors, and we spun these yarns and tales like you wouldn't believe to all the girls that we spoke to.

Zen was the first one to catch it. I wasn't there when he caught it, but obviously it featured quite heavily in the magazine. Then Phil caught it on a night I was there, and it was quite a funny night actually. I was expecting everybody to be together, but they weren't. I tried calling Steve, Phil and everybody, but no one was answering their phones. I guessed that they weren't fishing, so I headed off to Snake Pit thinking that if anyone was anywhere, that was where they're going to be. Steve said he wouldn't be at Johnsons, but in fact that's where he ended up. I went down to the Snake Pit and pulled into the car park. There was a car in there that I didn't

Harefield and back together again.

Nelson, a new lake record.

The Parrot looking after my rods while I'm up the pub.

Haulin'.

Stu Gillham haulin' too.

"Come on son, get the Mainline T shirt in the shot," Zen and Rael.

I christened it, "The Chinese Common".

Jon, always double awesome.

Essentials for a weekend session.

recognise and a guy fishing at the back of the school on the first bank round to the left.

I didn't particularly want to socialise so I cut round to the right and down into the Dugout swim where Zen had caught the forty. I sat there and got some spots sorted out. It was about seven o'clock and I thought, well, why break with tradition? I'll go down the pub on my own… Who knows, there might be some people down there that I recognise. There weren't as it turned out, and I got a absolutely rat-arsed, and ended up in a pub quite close to the Snake Pit having a fight with the band who were playing that night, and it broke out onto the street. I say a fight, but it was a big argument with a lot of pushing and shoving by this big, fat drunk bloke who was missing his mates. I ended up staggering back to the lake on my own and slinging them out into the middle of snags. I was awoken in the morning by the thunder of footsteps behind me, and lo and behold it was Phil Harper. He had been there the night before, but was in a different vehicle to what he normally drove. I told him that I'd been out on my own that night and what had happened, and he laughed and said, "Well, tonight we'll make up for it; we'll go out the pair of us."

So we went out and we had a fantastic night on the Saturday night, Phil and I, down in Colchester. I think we were brain surgeons that night, and whether the girls believed us or not, I don't know, but we had the crack anyway. We came back to the lake, had a few beers in Phil's swim and cast them out to God knows where. Next morning at seven o'clock, Phil was back in my swim. "I've got it, mate!" I couldn't believe it; the Snake Pit common at 41lb, and on a pub chuck as well. Good angling, mate. "Catch them on your own terms," was our motto, and still is to this day. Famous Five forever.

So basically we were here there and everywhere, and we didn't know whether to fish Johnsons. We quite fancied it; I mean Steve wanted to catch the Leather. I'd caught it, so I didn't really want to go back up there – there was nothing in there that I really wanted to catch. It was a long way for Phil to go, and why would he go all the way up there when he'd got the Snake Pit on his doorstep and that forty in there?

The Colne Valley was beckoning us back, not to Savay of course, but to the lake directly behind Savay, Pit 3, owned by Gerrards Cross, which was an unknown quantity. There were rumours of really big fish in there, but none of us had ever known anyone who had fished there, and we didn't know what was in there. So we had a few sessions over there, and I think Phil ended up with an 18 or a 20. I think Steve had a 22 or 23, and I think Dave Whibley had had a 20 as well. I never had a bite on there though; I just couldn't get a bite.

We'd had the odd trip to Farlows in the closed season; it was a good crack over there. I'll tell you some of the stories that happened over there shortly, but a lake that was really going from strength to strength was Harefield Lake on the Boyer Leisure ticket. John Stent, who was based down at Farlows, was the controller of all the lakes. They had some good lakes; they had Rodney Meadow with fish to upper 30s, a fish called Big Rod, which funnily enough disappeared around this time and was never seen again. They also had Willow Pool, and I remember an early article in Big Carp from Phil Thompson who had been fishing Willow. They had some good fish in there up around the 30lb mark including Nelson, the one-eyed carp.

Then they had the big water, Harefield Lake, directly opposite the Horse and Barge pub, and John wanted to create another Savay. If anything he wanted to create a water better than Savay. He was never going to succeed, that's for sure, but he had a damn good try at it. He netted and electro-fished virtually all his other waters, took out all the carp and all but a couple of 30s, which he put into Farlows (it might have only been one, the Pet, I think it was called), went into Harefield. Suddenly this water went from a low stocked 50-acre gravel pit to a runs water, but the runs were from 20lb-plus fish. It had probably around 20 different thirties in it, which for 1990/91 was amazing, not far off of what Savay had in it. It had a huge head of 20s as well, probably a hundred other fish in there, doubles and twenties, and a lot of high 20s as well.

Of course I went on to have some really good fun there, I've got to say. It was the lake where we all suddenly found ourselves back together again. We all wanted to fish Harefield, John Stent kindly let us fish there together again, and it was fantastic to be back in the Colne Valley. It was almost as good as fishing Savay again; we were still going to the Horse and Barge, still going up to Abu's for our curry, and still having a massive laugh there with the guys from the other lakes in the Colne Valley, so socially, it was just as good. There's only one Savay, and those of you lucky enough to have fished Savay will know what I mean. It is a very, very special water and there will only ever be one Savay, but Harefield was good.

It was great for us as well, and it was all very much a learning curve again. It was a big gravel pit and we'd been fishing small pits so we weren't kitted out for fishing 120 yards out. None of us had the rods or reels, so we all had to step up our gear and change everything from lines to hooks. Luckily I still had my wonder pop-ups, my legendary little orange pop-ups, which absolutely slaughtered Harefield over the couple of years I was on there.

Most of you have probably seen the films I made on there, The Harefield

Video cover carp.

Big Robbie.

Ritchie Mac gives Briggsy a hand.

Roll on pub time!

Steve with the Big Fully, on my bait!

The pop-ups are doing it.

And one off the top too.

Hauling videos. They were great fun and we caught a lot of fish for that, Stuart Gillham and I. It was the lake that I met Stuart on, and that I met Knacker on, and I made some good new friends down there. There was also Essex Jon of course, and he and I became best buddies. We joined a fair way through the season, maybe sort of September time, and I remember one of my first sessions down there, if not my first, getting set up on the Road Bank by the round island and seeing some fish moving on the other side of a bar. I'd been told by a couple of the guys we'd met there, Frogger and Care Bear, that there was a shallow bar off the island, and if I was lucky enough to get a bite, I would need to walk the fish to the right to get it over the bar. We'd set up after lunch on a Friday afternoon, pinged the rods out for a couple of hours before we were back over to the Horse and Barge again, and lo and behold, away it went. I had a 27 or 28lb common, one of the original commons, and what a great start that was.

Well, I can't leave Harefield without telling you some of the funny stories that went on there. I remember one particular occasion Paul Selman coming and fishing a couple of swims down from me and catching a thirty. Now if you caught a big'un on Harefield, it was only good manners to buy a round of drinks. Of course I went down and told Paul this, but being the tight-arsed northern bugger that he is, he said, "Oh no man, I haven't got any money." So I said, "Well don't worry about that, I'll stand you in at the bar; you go up there and be the big man and get the drinks in." So we led him over there, put him up at the bar and one by one the guys were coming in off the lake. Paul was shouting back, "My shout, my shout," and of course one by one he was buying the drinks. Then just before he'd finished, he asked me what I wanted, and I got my pint of lager. He got himself a drink, then turned round and the barman said, "£35.50," so Paul turned round to me and said, "£35.50." I said, "Yeah," and he said, "Well, come on then, you were going to stand me in." I replied, "No, I said I'd stand up at the bar with you." It was very embarrassing for Paul, and I think they ended up putting it on a tab for him and he sorted it out next time he was there.

The Horse and Barge was the gathering place for anglers all over the Colne Valley, but it was also a very popular pub with the pretty girls of the area, and with people like Phil Harper and Essex Jon amongst us, there was plenty of pulling going on and girls being brought back to the lake. There were also some fantastic nightclubs in the area, and very often we'd end up at Paradise Lost in Watford or up at Abu's, the local Indian restaurant. There' are far too many funny stories associated with Abu's but one of the funniest I remember was a night we had up there with Albert Romp, Stuart Gillham and the rest of the Harefield guys. About 30 of us took a long table and with only two little Indian guys serving and cooking, we were obviously going to be in there for a long while, so plenty of drinking was going on.

I was sat next to Stuart Gillham on my right hand side and Albert on my left on this particular occasion, and Stuart was packing a plastic bag into the pocket of his coat. I asked him what was in it, and he said it was raw mincemeat for his little dog that he'd got with him. I had a look in this plastic bag and there was this sort of very fatty raw mince. Now Albert to my left was being a bit of a nuisance; he kept sticking his hand in any food that arrived on the table and grabbing a handful and eating it. This was not his own food by the way – any bit of naan bread that came along he'd pull a lump off, or if a tray of Bombay potatoes went up the table, in his hand would go and grab a handful of it and stick it in his gob.

Well, I thought I'd have a bit of fun with Albert, so I asked Stuart if I could have the dog mince. Taking one of the little silver trays that the Indian food came in, I squashed about 1lb of this dog mince and then tipped the remainder of a vindaloo sauce that someone had left on the table over the top. I strategically pushed it out in front, baiting a swim in front of Albert. He had been looking down the table to see what other tasty morsels were

The Pink Linear, one of the A-Team.

L.S.A. CHAMPION-OF-THE-SEASON 1989/90

All Senior and Junior Catch-of-the-Month winners were invited to Thorpe Park on 19th November, 1989 to receive their prizes and to enjoy a days fishing.

Although the Pike fishing did not live up to expectations a good day was had by all. The overall total weight of fish caught was 227.lbs.2.ozs.

Whilst most people chose to fish for Pike, Peter Dovey used quiver-tip and swimfeeder tactics. Bites were slow to start but he persevered and managed to catch an excellent bag of quality Roach and Bream to take the title.

Final adjudication of catches made on the day:

L.S.A. SENIOR CHAMPION OF THE SEASON 1989/90

PETER DOVEY - 31.lbs.11.oz.

L.S.A. JUNIOR CHAMPION OF THE SEASON 1989/90

GARY DOWNING - 20.lbs.13.oz.

Both winners received a trophy, together with additional prizes of £200 and £100 for the Senior and Junior winners respectively.

CATCH-OF-THE-MONTH COMPETITION 1990/91

MONTHLY PRIZE WINNERS
All prize winners will be notified of their success, but prizes will not be distributed immediately. At the end of the season, all 10 Senior and 10 Junior winners, will be invited to take part in the final match to be held at Thorpe Park. Prizes won during the season will be presented at the end of this match by a well-known personality.

The Senior and Junior winners of the match on that day, will be declared L.S.A. CHAMPION OF THE SEASON and will be presented with a trophy and additional prizes. Attendance or participation in this match is not of course, compulsory and those not wishing to take part will receive their monthly prize after this match has been held.

CATCH-OF-THE-MONTH WINNER – DECEMBER 1989

My personal best by Jock White.
I went up to Yateley on Friday the 15th December to fish for the weekend and on arriving there instead of going to the lake that I had been spending a fair bit of time on this season, I decided to fish the Pad Lake from which I had an amazing result last winter, when on my first trip on that lake, I had three fish up to 31.lb.13.oz.

I chose to fish the same swim that I had my result from almost a year ago and on getting all the tackle set up about mid afternoon I fired out about 100 free baits, all round the edge of a bed of lillies, about 30 yards out from where I was fishing, then I cast out both rods.

The following morning after I had a re-cast, the right hand rod went off at 10.45 am, and I was into a fish. It had gone through some pads and when I pulled it back through them there was a big swirl. The fish then began to take some line as it moved towards the middle of the lake. When I managed to stop it, it began kiting right. It headed for the branches that were hanging in the water to my right about 35 yards away. It went solid for a minute or so and as I put a bit more bend in the rod I felt the fish start to move. It came along the bank nice and steady and just a few yards to my right in front of some reeds the fish showed itself tor the first time, and I saw that it was a real good fish. A couple of minutes later it slipped into the landing net.

When I put on the scales the needle went round to 40.lb.10.oz. and I let out a loud YA-HOO! I had done my personal best once more on the Yateley complex.

MELVIN (JOCK) WHITE with his magnificent Mirror Carp of 40.lbs.10.oz. from the Yateley venue.

ACCESS, BARCLAY CARD VISA SERVICE

Members who wish to use this system to purchase their permits etc. must complete the appropriate section of the Permit Application form stating their Access/Barclay Card/Visa Number. DO NOT SEND YOUR CARD.

This facility can only be used for application made direct to L.S.A. at Thorpe Park, and is NOT available at permit agencies. We regret that this offer is for mail order only and no telephone ordering system is available.

BARCLAY CARD/VISA
Members using this particular card, are advised that the authorisation system employed by this Company, causes a further delay of up to an extra 10 days in supplying their permit.

CATCH-OF-THE-MONTH, 1989

MONTH	SENIOR WINNER	SPECIES	WEIGHT	JUNIOR WINNER	SPECIES	WEIGHT
January	D. Wood	Chub	5- 4-0	L. Jenkins	Pike	20- 0-0
February	I. Russell	Chub	6- 2-0	J. Claridge	Pike	23- 8-0
March	P. Dovey	Barbel	11- 4-0		No Entry	
June	N. Lee	Carp	44- 8-0	A. Blight	Bream	7- 2-0
July	C. Hobden	Perch	3- 2-0	D. Oliver	Carp	23- 8-0
August	B. Obourn	Carp	43- 8-0	A. Blight	Carp	25- 6-0
September	D. Orriss	Carp	40-12-0	D. Fellows	Carp	29- 0-0
October	S. Bown	Carp	43- 4-0	M. French	Carp	26- 6-0
November	C. Fox	Pike	30- 0-0	J. McKie	Pike	23- 8-0
December	M. White	Carp	40-10-0	L. Minton	Pike	24-14-0

Extract from the Leisure Sport Echo Sounder depicting Jock (or Melvin – ha ha!) White with Jumbo at 40lb 10oz. See also in the list Don Orris with Heather at 40lb 12oz.

6 STONELEIGH COURT,
FRIMLEY,
CAMBERLEY,
SURREY
GU16 5XH

19th February 1991

Dear Rob,

Hello, how are you? Well I hope . . . and as I here, going into the
Publishing Business in a *Big Way!*. Best of luck with this venture, it's
got to be better than designing Lorries, I think! The printing world in
general is <u>not</u> a good business to be in anymore from my point of view, I
can't make the real super money I used too. Still, why am I telling you
all this trivia, god only knows.

However, back to matters on the fishing front, You'll find enclosed with
this letter a new updated list of mine *'The Big Carp List'*. As you can see
it catalogues all Carp reported over 40Ib. caught in the U.K. It's been
running sometime now - stuff like this interests me greatly - it seems not
many people around are bothered to keep this information. Although
everybody wants this kind of statistical info. on tap, so to speak. To me,
we must keep this list and naturally enough it must be as accurate as
possible. Here, there will always be problems, as we in the 'Carp World'
are often subjected to hearsay, rumours and darn-right lies!

I need your help, Rob. Can you look carefully at this list and change,
add, delete or correct any of the entries. For instance, can you help with
information on the *'Springwell'* captures of this last year, 11 forty pound+
captures I believe, coming from Four different carp, if this is so it's
the first water to produce 'Four Forties' in our History. Your contacts in
the 'Valley' are better than mine (they might not want to tell me anyway!)

Items of note that you might be interested in . . . Richard Lloyd's 46Ib
12oz fish I know is genuine . . . but its capture is fraught with problems
. . . *He Stole It*. It now lives somewhere else in Surrey, and the bugger
has recaught it again last year, although I don't know the weight.

The 'Kingsmead' fish has been more or less confirmed by my contacts within
Leisure Sport. Although I will investigate further, as it still sounds a
bit suspect.

Please keep this information to yourself as it taken me sometime to
compile, when its completed, by the close season I'll send you the update.
Look forward to hearing from you, and keep up the good work,

TELEPHONE: 0276 21735

Letter and big carp list from Chris Ball 1991 asking me to verify certain captures.

Big Carp List
40lb Plus Carp

	Weight	Captor	Location	Date
A	51-08-0 (M)	Chris Yates	Redmire Pool	June 1980
	46-12-0 (M)	Richard Lloyd	Surrey Pond	March 1990
B	46-02-0 (L)	Pete Richards	Fennymere	August 1989
C	45-12-0 (M)	Ritchie McDonald	Yateley North Lake	October 1984
C	45-08-0 (M)	Tony Moore	Yateley North Lake	July 1990
	45-08-0 (M)	Albert Romp	Savay	June 1990
B	45-02-0 (L)	Ray Stone	Fennymere	December 1986
B	45-00-0 (L)	Mark Fitzpatrick	Fennymere	June 1989
B	45-00-0 (L)	Mark Fitzpatrick	Fennymere	July 1989
B	45-00-0 (L)	Ray Stone	Fennymere	July 1987
B	44-14-0 (L)	Ray Stone	Fennymere	November 1986
B	44-12-0 (L)	Keith Longden	Fennymere	August 1987
C	44-08-0 (M)	Graham Mountain	Yateley North Lake	March 1989
C	44-08-0 (M)	Nick Lee	Yateley North Lake	1989
	44-06-0 (M)	Ray Greenwood	Henlow Grange	June 1984
D	44-04-0 (M)	Steve Allcot	Longfield	December 1989
C	44-04-0 (M)	Dave Baker	Yateley North Lake	1985
B	44-00-0 (L)	Mark Fitzpatrick	Fennymere	June 1987
	44-00-0 (C)	Richard Walker	Redmire Pool	September 1952
I	44-00-0 (M)	Steve Burgess	Horton	June 1990
	43-13-8 (C)	Chris Yates	Redmire Pool	August 1972
B	43-08-0 (L)	Ray Stone	Fennymere	September 1985
E	43-08-0 (L)	Keith O'Conner	Springwell	October 1984
C	43-08-0 (M)	Brian O'Bourn	Yateley North Lake	1989
C	43-04-0 (M)	Steve Brown	Yateley North Lake	October 1989
C	43-04-0 (M)	Adrian Tilbury	Yateley North Lake	July 1984
B	43-04-0 (L)	Gary Morgan	Fennymere	August 1986
C	43-04-0 (M)	Sam Fox	Yateley North Lake	September 1984
C	43-04-0 (M)	Ray Fuller	Yateley North Lake	July 1987
G	43-04-0 (M)	Clive Gibbins	Sandholme Pool	1984
	43-04-0 (M)	AN Other	Kingsmead	July 1990
M	43-01-0 (M)	Peter Bond	Yateley Pads Lake	November 1990
	43-00-0 (M)*	Graham Mountian	Trilakes	1983
L	43-00-0 (M)	Jonathan Leigh	Surrey Club Lake	July 1980
C	42-12-0 (M)	Kerry Barringer	Yateley North Lake	1985
	42-12-0 (L)	Martin Symonds	Waltham Abbey	September 1976
I	42-12-0 (M)	Bernard Blight	Horton	August 1990
C	42-08-0 (M)	Nick Peat	Yateley North Lake	1985
	42-08-0 (M)	Bob Copeland	Springwell	June 1990
B	42-06-0 (L)	Vic Bailey	Fennymere	June 1985
	42-04-0 (M)	Max Cottis	Savay	June 1990
B	42-04-0 (L)	Mark Fitzpatrick	Fennymere	October 1984

	Weight	Captor	Location	Date
B	42-04-0 (L)	Ray Stone	Fennymere	July 1986
	42-02-0 (C)	John Lilley	Mangrove	1988
C	42-00-0 (M)	Mark Lawson	Yateley North Lake	1989
D	42-00-0 (M)	John Allen	Longfield	December 1987
	42-00-0 (M)	Ray Clay	Billing Aquadrome	September 1966
	42-00-0 (M)	Ken Hodder	Yateley Car Park Lake	October 1979
E	42-00-0 (L)	Zen Boiko	Springwell	1984
D	42-00-0 (M)	Terry Dempsey	Longfield	September 1989
D	42-00-0 (M)	Jon Holt	Longfield	August 1987
	41-12-0 (M)	Thomas Gelston	Hainault	November 1985
D	41-12-0 (M)	Dave Whibley	Longfield	1989
K	41-12-0 (M)	Alan Taylor	Mid-Northants	June 1990
C	41-10-0 (M)	Jan Wenczka	Yateley North Lake	August 1981
F	41-08-0 (C)	David Westerman	Snake Pit, Essex	June 1988
O	41-08-0 (L)	Robin Dix	Yateley Car Park Lake	June 1985
J	41-08-0 (M)	Kevin Nash	Silver End Pit	June 1985
	41-08-0 (M)	Alan	Standstead Abbott	December 1989
F	41-08-0 (C)	Phil Harper	Snake Pit, Essex	September 1989
C	41-05-0 (M)	Chris Riddington	Yateley North Lake	October 1980
L	41-00-0 (M)	Jonathan Leigh	Surrey Club Lake	October 1978
B	41-00-0 (L)	Mark Fitzpatrick	Fennymere	September 1984
	41-00-0 (M)	Peter Wilson	Withy Pool	June 1990
	41-00-0 (M)		Mid-Northants	June 1990
K	40-12-0 (M)	Dave MacIntyre	Mid-Northants	October 1989
O	40-12-0 (L)	Don Orriss	Yateley Car Park Lake	October 1989
	40-12-0 (M)	Steve Hale	MOD Aldermaston	1987
M	40-10-0 (M)	Jock White	Yateley Pads Lake	1989
H	40-10-0 (M)	Jon Holt	Longfield	1982
G	40-08-0 (M)	Kevin Clifford	Sandholme Pool	1983
A	40-08-0 (M)	Eddie Price	Redmire Pool	September 1959
H	40-08-0 (M)	Colin Swaden	Longfield	1980
F	40-08-0 (C)	Zen Boiko	Snake Pit, Essex	1988
E	40-08-0 (L)	Bernie Stamp	Sprincjwell	July 1987
	40-08-0 (M)	Dave Cumpstone	Wraysbury	June 1990
I	40-08-0 (M)	Geoff Ball	Horton	September 1990
	40-04-0 (M)	Richard Johnson	Longfield	1985
	40-04-0	AN Other	Pit 2	June 1988
G	40-04-0 (M)	Kevin Clifford	Sandholme Pool	1984
	40-04-0 (M)	Nick West	Wraysbury	1980
J	40-04-0 (M)	Phil Harper	Silver End Pit	1984
K	40-04-0 (M)	Alan Taylor	Mid-Northants	January 1989
K	40-04-0 (M)	Kevin Maddocks	Mid-Northants	January 1990
A	40-03-0 (M)	Jack Hilton	Redmire Pool	July 1972
H	40-03-0 (M)	Colin Swaden	Longfield	1980
E	40-02-0 (L)	Paul Fickling	Springwell	1985

	Weight	Captor	Location	Date
D	40-02-0 (M)	John Allen	Longfield	July 1988
D	40-02-0 (M)	Matthew McKwen	Longfield	July 1989
	40-02-0 (M)	Allan Partridge	Springwell	September 1990
	40-00-8 (M)	Ron Groombridge	Boxmoor	June 1966
B	40-00-0 (L)	Ian Longden	Fennymere	September 1984
A	40-00-0 (M)	John MacLeod	Redmire Pool	July 1972
	40-00-0 (M)	Henry Weeks	Peckham	July 1972
D	40-00-0 (M)	Clive Williams	Longfield	August 1988
K	40-00-0 (M)	Steve Gombocz	Mid-Northants	February 1990

Big Carp List
40lb Plus Carp – Individual Fish

Fish A

A	40-08-0 (M)	Eddie Price	Redmire Pool	September 1959
A	40-03-0 (M)	Jack Hilton	Redmire Pool	July 1972
A	40-00-0 (M)	John MacLeod	Redmire Pool	July 1972
A	51-08-0 (M)	Chris Yates	Redmire Pool	June 1980

Fish B

B	40-00-0 (L)	Ian Longden	Fennymere	September 1984
B	41-00-0 (L)	Mark Fitzpatrick	Fennymere	September 1984
B	42-04-0 (L)	Mark Fitzpatrick	Fennymere	October 1984
B	42-06-0 (L)	Vic Bailey	Fennymere	June 1985
B	43-08-0 (L)	Ray Stone	Fennymere	September 1985
B	42-04-0 (L)	Ray Stone	Fennymere	July 1986
B	43-04-0 (L)	Gary Morgan	Fennymere	August 1986
B	44-14-0 (L)	Ray Stone	Fennymere	November 1986
B	45-02-0 (L)	Ray Stone	Fennymere	December 1986
B	44-00-0 (L)	Mark Fitzpatrick	Fennymere	June 1987
B	45-00-0 (L)	Ray Stone	Fennymere	July 1987
B	44-12-0 (L)	Keith Longden	Fennymere	August 1987
B	45-00-0 (L)	Mark Fitzpatrick	Fennymere	June 1989
B	45-00-0 (L)	Mark Fitzpatrick	Fennymere	July 1989
B	46-02-0 (L)	Pete Richards	Fennymere	August 1989

Fish C

C	41-05-0 (M)	Chris Riddington	Yateley North Lake	October 1980
C	41-10-0 (M)	Jan Wenczka	Yateley North Lake	August 1981
C	43-04-0 (M)	Adrian Tilbury	Yateley North Lake	July 1984
C	43-04-0 (M)	Sam Fox	Yateley North Lake	September 1984
C	45-12-0 (M)	Ritchie McDonald	Yateley North Lake	October 1984
C	44-04-0 (M)	Dave Baker	Yateley North Lake	1985
C	42-12-0 (M)	Kerry Barringer	Yateley North Lake	1985
C	42-08-0 (M)	Nick Peat	Yateley North Lake	1985

C	43-04-0 (M)	Ray Fuller	Yateley North Lake	July 1987
C	44-08-0 (M)	Graham Mountain	Yateley North Lake	March 1989
C	44-08-0 (M)	Nick Lee	Yateley North Lake	1989
C	43-08-0 (M)	Brian O'Bourn	Yateley North Lake	1989
C	42-00-0 (M)	Mark Lawson	Yateley North Lake	1989
C	46-08-0 (M)	Tony Moore	Yateley North Lake	July 1990

Fish D*

D	42-00-0 (M)	Jon Holt	Longfield	August 1987
D	42-00-0 (M)	John Allen	Longfield	December 1987
D	40-02-0 (M)	John Allen	Longfield	July 1988
D	40-00-0 (M)	Clive Williams	Longfield	August 1988
D	41-12-0 (M)	Dave Whibley	Longfield	1989
D	40-02-0 (M)	Matthew McKwen	Longfield	July 1989
D	42-00-0 (M)	Terry Dempsey	Longfield	September 1989
D	44-04-0 (M)	Steve Allcot	Longfield	December 1989

Fish E

E	40-04-0 (L)	Lee Jackson	Springwell	1983
E	43-08-0 (L)	Keith O'Conner	Springwell	October 1984
E	42-00-0 (L)	Zen Boiko	Springwell	1984
E	40-08-0 (L)	Bernie Stamp	Springwell	July 1987

Fish F

F	41-08-0 (C)	David Westerman	Snake Pit, Essex	June 1988
F	40-08-0 (C)	Zen Boiko	Snake Pit, Essex	1988
F	41-08-0 (C)	Phil Harper	Snake Pit, Essex	September 1989

Fish G

G	40-08-0 (M)	Kevin Clifford	Sandholme Pool	1983
G	43-04-0 (M)	Clive Gibbins	Sandholme Pool	1984
G	40-04-0 (M)	Kevin Clifford	Sandholme Pool	1984

Fish H

H	40-08-0 (M)	Colin Swaden	Longfield	1980
H	40-03-0 (M)	Colin Swaden	Longfield	1980
H	40-10-0 (M)	Jon Holt	Longfield	1982

Fish I *

I	44-00-0 (M)	Steve Burgess	Horton	June 1990
I	42-12-0 (M)	Bernard Blight	Horton	August 1990
I	40-08-0 (M)	Geoff Ball	Horton	September 1990

Fish J

J	40-04-0 (M)	Phil Harper	Silver End Pit	1984
J	41-08-0 (M)	Kevin Nash	Silver End Pit	June 1985

Fish K				
K	40-04-0 (M)	Alan Taylor	Mid-Northants	January 1989
K	40-12-0 (M)	Dave MacIntyre	Mid-Northants	October 1989
K	40-04-0 (M)	Kevin Maddocks	Mid-Northants	January 1990
K	40-00-0 (M)	Steve Gombocz	Mid~Northants	February 1990
K	41-12-0 (M)	Alan Taylor	Mid-Northants	June 1990
Fish L				
L	41-00-0 (M)	Jonathan Leigh	Surrey Club Lake	October 1978
L	43-00-0 (M)	Jonathan Leigh	Surrey Club Lake	July 1980
Fish M				
M	40-10-0 (M)	Jock White	Yateley Pads Lake	1989
M	43-01-0 (M)	Peter Bond	Yateley Pads Lake	November 1990

coming along, and suddenly spotted this tray of curry in front of him. In went his hands and out came a great big dollop of raw dog mince covered in vindaloo sauce, straight into Albert's mouth. I peed myself with laughter as did Stuart. We thought he must soon realise that he was eating something cold and raw but he didn't, and do you know what? He ate the whole tray – a least 1lb of raw, fatty dog mince covered in vindaloo sauce.

I think that night almost everybody sat at that table was ill for one reason or another, but the only person who wasn't ill was Albert, a man of iron constitution. Albert was a fantastic character. He had everybody in stitches wherever he went, and I've mentioned a few of his funny stories in my books before. But he did meet his match one day when we were at a carp fishing meeting in Hatfield and who should be there but Jim Davidson, professional comedian and also a keen carp angler. Jim decided to give us a few jokes up on the stage, and Albert was his number one heckler. Every time Jim said something, Albert would butt in with his little funny quip and have the people around him in stitches. Now Jim Davison is certainly not the one to mess with when it comes to heckling; he must have worked some of the hardest clubs around the country, and Albert was going to be easy meat for him. I remember Jim Davison about to say something about his mother-in-law when Albert blurted something out again, and with that, Jim Davidson stopped speaking, turned round and looked at Albert. Albert looked at him and Jim said, "Do you know what? That's the first time I've seen a pig standing on its hands drinking lager through its arse!" With that we all creased up laughing, as Albert had been well and truly stitched – the first time and last time ever.

The fishing on Harefield was fast and furious, and so were our nights out. In 1991, I finished my campaign on Harefield in style by doing a double box set of videos with an old mate of mine, Len Gurd, the Harefield Haulin' tapes, which featured Stuart Gillham and me. Oh what fantastic fishing we had at that opening week. We had chosen our swims some weeks before, and as I was using Nash bait at the time, Kevin graciously allowed me to have as much bait as I wanted to bait up Harefield before the filming was going to take place. So Stuart Gillham, who was using a lot of hemp at the time, went up there with his lilo and was tipping in half hundred weight sacks of hemp every week, and I was walking up there with a rucksack full of boilies once a week for the three weeks leading up to our filming. It was the best baiting up campaign I have ever done in my life, and it meant that most of the fish in the lake were up in that area come June 16th. If my memory serves me right, I had 42 takes over that first week period and landed about 26 fish, nigh on all of them 20lb-plus with a few 30s thrown in as well, including a fantastic pink linear, one of the most sought after fish in Harefield.

That season I had also opened my account on Harefield, with the first fish of the season being a new lake record – Nelson at 38lb-plus, doubling up with Essex Jon in the first swim on the Broadwater Bank. Jon and I had had a wager not half an hour before, with some prize money for the first fish of our session and for the biggest fish. We were far too drunk to cast

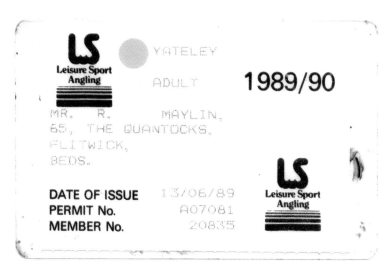

Yateley's calling.

out that night when we got back, but finally rose from our beds about 9am and slung them out. Five minutes later I had a new lake record on the bank and took the money for both prizes from Jon. Good angling.

Stuart Gillham and Jon continued fishing Harefield when I left. I decided that enough was enough after doing the Harefield Hauling videos; I caught the majority of the fish that I was after. There was a complex of lakes down in Surrey that had taken my attention over a period of time, and the time was now right for me to descend upon these lakes. Earlier that year I had presented another video for the Yateley Yahoo Crew, depicting all their great captures over the years on this complex. Now it was my turn to move onto Yateley and to catch some of its famous residents. The hunt for Bazil had begun!

Chapter 6

A Change for the Better — Pursuit of the Dream Water

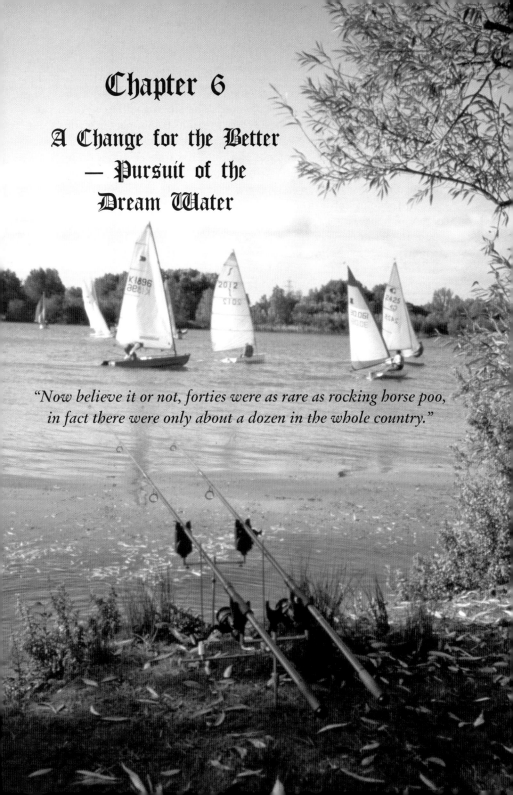

"Now believe it or not, forties were as rare as rocking horse poo, in fact there were only about a dozen in the whole country."

My times at Harefield were great times indeed. The Famous Five were back together again, singing our theme song, 'We catch them here, we catch them there, we catch them mirrors everywhere'. The Horse and Barge, Abu's, the nightclubs – great times. With the closed seasons being spent at Farlows, it was a full-on party for 12 months of the year. But sadly, as they say, everything must come to an end. Nothing lasts forever, and after making my Harefield Haulin' videos with my good old friend Stuart Gillham, I decided that enough was enough and that I was to be Hampshire bound, onwards and upwards in search of a forty.

Now believe it or not, in those times forties were as rare as rocking horse poo. In fact I believe there were only about a dozen throughout the whole country. That seems unbelievable today sitting here writing this, as there are literally dozens of fifties, and I probably know of almost as many sixties that have been caught in this country as there were forties then. In fact in last week's angling press, in one of the weekly papers, I counted no less than 48 different 40lb carp that had been caught that week – that's how much things have changed. For the better or for the worse, I'm going to let you be the judge of that.

Anyway, Big Carp magazine had been going for a year or so and was well established in the carp fishing market. It was very, very well received by carp anglers all over the world and within the first year, the magazine was already being sent out to half a dozen different countries, and was very popular in the UK, solely distributed through fishing tackle shops, as I hadn't yet branched out into the news trade. With a frequency of only one magazine every two months, it left me with ample time on my hands to concentrate on some of the hard venues around the Yateley area; venues with a formidable reputation and with a line-up of good anglers fishing each of the lakes in search of the legendary inhabitants.

The lake that I had always fancied concentrating on, and had in some small manner tackled in previous years, having fished the odd session, was the North Lake, and of course the fish I was after was the one and only Bazil, so I decided to move from Harefield and concentrate on Yateley. A couple of my friends decided that they would also fish down that way with me – Phil Harper for one, and Martin Locke in a small way. The three of us began fishing the North Lake with our normal style of catching them on our own terms, spending the day on the lake and the nights in the nightclubs. This had always been our style of fishing, and I'm afraid to say we weren't going to change, not for any fish, even one with such a formidable reputation as Bazil, and that's probably why it took me two years to catch it. My captures on these lakes have been well written about in

Bazil's Bush and One Last Cast, two of my titles written previously, which contain all the details of the fish that I caught while fishing these fantastic venues.

These books also contain a chapter on Stanstead Abbots where a fortuitous session, brought about because both Heather and Bazil had just been caught, resulted in me putting my name on one of the most gorgeous carp in the country.

As those of you who have followed my career will know, I didn't just stop on the North Lake after catching Bazil. It was then on to the Pad Lake after Jumbo, then the Car Park Lake, then Swan Valley, Frimley, Horseshoe and Sandhurst. Although I will speak a little of the captures on these venues, most of it has been written about before, and I don't intend going over all the old ground again. What I would like to do however is tell you about some of the other things that happened, which haven't been written about, and some of the friendships I forged fishing these great venues.

I've always made good friends wherever I've fished. I'm still in contact with some of the guys from Arlesey when I fished there in the 70s and early 80s. Likewise the North Harrow Waltonians – some friends from there are still in contact with me to this day. Savay of course speaks for itself; the camaraderie on the Looney Rota was second to none, and although I only see most of these guys two or three times a year, mostly at the shows, it's as though we've never been apart. I think what sums up a great friendship is when you don't need to see somebody every week, but as soon as you do see them, catch up with what's been going on and reminisce about old times, it's as though the two of you have never been apart. That's the feeling I get with the likes of Steve Allcott, Dave Whibley, Martin Locke, Colin Martin… the list goes on. I mean so many great friendships were made over the years.

Certainly one of the most fantastic things about carp fishing are these friendships that you form, and Yateley was no exception. I don't really think I was looking for any more friends; I've got more than enough, but just being on the lake all the time and being around these guys, you meet friends who have certain traits and certain idiosyncrasies, certain things about them that bring the two of you together. If it's a true friendship then it will stand the test of time even if you don't see each other for a while.

Among the friendships that I formed down at Yateley was Glyn Goodger, a guy from Essex who I met down on the banks of the Car Park Lake. He became a great friend of mine and was the best man at my wedding in 2004. Even to this day, the two of us speak every week on the telephone. He was a really good clubbing mate of mine as well; we had some fantastic times together. Glyn still fishes every week – he's as passionate about it as

Don Orris with Heather.

Maylin's from Stanstead Abbots.

Now a mid-forty.

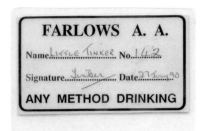

My tickets for this era.

Carp Society News 1994.

Jock with Bazil.

Bernie, Sandy and crew at Farlows.

The ballet dancer.

The Dustbin off the top.

Bazil, September 1993.

The Pad Lake's Scale on the Shoulder.

Pad Lake 35.

Rob McGill with Henry.

Henry.

Pad Lake 35.

we ever were. In fact he fishes more than I do these days.

Another great friend of mine who I met on the banks of Yateley was Rob McGill. Rob and I fished together a lot, and it's sad to report that as I write this piece, Rob is in a very bad way indeed. A few months ago, he was only given six months to live, and probably by the time this book comes out, Rob won't be with us any more. I would like to dedicate this book to Rob, a great friend of mine who helped me through some difficult times. We had some fantastic laughs together and enjoyed our fishing on a variety of waters, as he fished not only on the Yateley venues with me, but also at Swan Valley, Frimley, Horseshoe and Sandhurst. Rest in peace, my old mate. I love you so much.

I'll never forget the day I met young Terry Hearn. Big Rob and I were on our way up to the Oak pub at the top of the road at Yateley when little Tel came out of the Match Lake car park in his Fort Escort, gave a couple of bleeps on the horn, and pulled over next to us, offering us a lift up the road. We'd heard about little Tel over the other side of the road, taking the Match Lake apart, and everyone talking about what a good little angler he was. Tel decided that he would come in and have a pint with us, and the three of us sat in the window of the pub together while Tel talked about his fishing over on the other side of the road where the boys fished and the fish were smaller. He told us that when he'd finished on the Match Lake, he intended to go up to the North Lake and fish with the men. From that point onwards, Tel and I became great friends, and he contributed to Big Carp for a number of years. I hope I helped him become the man he is today; the most successful carp angler this country has ever known, and a really lovely guy as well. My time spent over on the Car Park Lake with Tel was one of the most enjoyable periods of my life, and I thank him for that.

Of course there were loads of other guys as well. The list would be far too long to mention them all here, but to all of you guys, thanks for all the memories and for the great part you played in my life; I really did have a great time at Yateley. So let me tell you about a few of the stories and the things that went on…

The first year I decided to fish the North Lake, I wanted to be on there for the start of the season. In those days there was a closed season, and we keenies used to get to the venue three or four days before the start of the season and camp out in the car park. I can't imagine why; it seems crazy sitting here writing about it now, but we did, and boy did we party in those three or four days before the off. We'd be in the pub lunchtimes and evenings, and by the time the start of the season actually came round, we were so knackered that we were almost ready to go home – we'd burned ourselves out before the season had even opened.

Come the start of that first season, there were quite a few good anglers fishing for Bazil. Jock White, the head of the Yahoo Crew had stamped his mark on the venue already, taking a couple of the other fish. Jock was on a roll and certainly the one to watch. I was taught a lesson that first year on the North Lake; I was the one following and they were the ones leading. There was a strange little character with very tight trousers, who we christened the Ballet Dancer, who caught a carp out of the North Lake every single time he went up there; he made us all look like idiots. I just couldn't put my finger on it; I thought I was doing everything right. I went on there with my legendary orange pop-ups, but they soon failed me, and I totally lost confidence in them.

I then began to jump from bait to bait, swapping from fishmeals to Robin Red to spice flavoured baits to meat flavoured baits to fish oils. I didn't know whether I was on my head or my arse. Every time I went up there the fish had been caught, and boy did the guys love to rub it in. The first capture of it that season was to the Ballet Dancer's mate, a boy called Leroy, whose biggest carp prior to catching Bazil was a double. The Ballet Dancer had lent him some of his boilies, and he'd gone into a swim in the corner of the lake where I'd never dreamt that Bazil would even venture, and caught it on his first night.

The next session I went up there, I pulled into the car park and big nosed Keith O'Sullivan turned round and said, "What are you doing here?" I said, "Well, I'm going on the North Lake," and he said, "Well, it's been out." It had been caught again from the 30/40 Swim, as it was then christened. I'm not sure of the captor, but once again Bazil had been out and made a fool out of me. It seemed like every time I went off the lake it was caught.

Jock White was next, and if my memory serves me right, it was then Johnny Darenth, who unfortunately committed suicide some years later. He was a lovely guy with a heart of gold, but obviously with a few problems at home, and it's sad to say he's no longer with us. I'm not sure whether it was Mickey Gray or Terry Pethybridge next, but Bazil came out four or five times that season. Everywhere I fished, it was caught in the opposite corner. In fact now my memory has come back to me, and it wasn't Leroy who caught it first, but in fact before that there was a capture out of the Corral on opening morning.

So anyway, I wasted my time totally that first year and decided after that humiliation that the following year wouldn't be the same. I would spend every available minute on the lake, even fishing on after it was caught. There was still a closed season, so that year the closed season was spent at Farlows,

Jumbo.

Motormouth with Arfur.

Chunky off the top.

My old mate John Lockwood.

Rainbow's end.

Chunky out of the Gate.

Car Park's Ugloe.

Wayne Dunn with Heather.

The mighty Arfur.

Floater fishing the Snag swim.

Pearly.

Got you, Single!

 **BRITISH RECORD (rod-caught) FISH COMMITTEE**

Our Ref: DR/LAJ/6

October 21, 1997

Mr. R.J. Maylin,
Bountyhunter Publications,
55 Broadhurst,
Farnborough,
Hants.
GU14 9XA.

Dear   Mr. Maylin.

We would be most grateful if you would kindly sign the enclosed British Record
(rod-caught) Fish Committee Witness to Weighing form in respect of the Carp
caught by Mr. Terry Hearn from Wraysbury last November.

A stamped addressed envelope is enclosed for your use and your immediate
attention to this matter would be greatly appreciated.

Thanking you.

Yours sincerely,

DAVID ROWE,
Secretary,
BRITISH RECORD (rod-caught) FISH COMMITTEE

British Record (rod-caught) Fish Committee
51A Queen Street, Newton Abbot, Devon, TQ12 2QJ (0626 331330)

Terry catches Mary at the British record weight and I am honoured to witness it.

He also caught Mallins.

Car Park's Big Common.

Chunk on the hemp.

Ugloe in the winter.

Dustbin in February.

The Orange in January.

and boy, the stories I could tell you about that place, but maybe even this is not the right place for those...

The following year I was back down there again. I'd made my mind up to fish Bazil's Bush as much as possible, as the fish had been caught out of there on a couple of occasions along with lots of other fish. Unfortunately in the draw, Rasta Andy drew that peg, and I ended up fishing the Car Park Lake. I actually made a swim on the end of the Works Bank so that I could be close to Bazil's Bush and keep an eye on the fish.

Rasta Andy and I became great friends, and he introduced me to that natural herb known as carp tobacco. Wow... the rest of it is a little hazy, but for a few years, Rasta and I were great friends and when in his company, and for that matter, when I wasn't, I was very chilled indeed. Let's leave it at that...

I'm glad to say that I kicked the smoking habit some four years ago now, and haven't had a cigarette, or anything else for that matter, in that period of time, but I wouldn't change anything for the world, and had a great time while I was doing it. I don't see Rasta Andy these days, but I'm sure he's out there somewhere, so cheers mate, and thanks for the good times.

I fished hard that year for Bazil, and it wasn't until September, in the Corral Swim funnily enough, that Bazil slipped up and made me the happiest guy in the world. I intended to do the trio of Bazil, Jumbo and Heather if possible, and decided that the Pad Lake should be my next port of call.

Unbeknown to me at the time, CEMEX Angling had plans to scrap the closed season, and for the first time ever, Yateley was open for 12 months of the year. I had a good year on the Pad Lake and ended up catching all the residents – a couple of the big ones more than once.

I'd met a young lady, a sister of a fishing friend of mine, and she spent a lot of time down at the lake with me. We had some good times, and some bad for that matter. I remember she had a white bull terrier called Buster, who was always great entertainment on the lake, and all the guys down there loved him. Sadly he's passed away now, but they were good times indeed.

After the Pad Lake and the capture of Jumbo in that first April of the open closed season, it was off to the Car Park Lake for one of the most enjoyable years in my fishing life. Young Terry Hearn was up one end of the lake and I was down the other, taking all the geese eggs and cooking great big omelettes with them. We had the local cafe delivering breakfast to the lake on a tray. The local Indian restaurant would let us go in there at midnight or one o'clock in the morning and after we'd finished eating he would take us back to the lake in his car. I've written about most of this in my last book One Last Cast, but it just seems incredible that we got away with so much.

Over these years my confrontations with Graham from the Environment Agency had continued. As you will recall I had run-ins with him at the North Harrow Waltonians, and the next time we crossed paths was actually at Harefield. I had purchased my rod licences from the shop at Farlows that year, as I was fishing there in the closed season, and had had them checked down there several times by Graham and other enforcement officers.

Come opening week of the season I was on Harefield, and who should turn up on opening day but Graham again? Do you know, I searched everywhere for those rod licences but never could find them, so Graham issued me with some paperwork to fill out where I'd purchased them from so that this could be verified and replacement licences issued to me. I informed the Environment Agency that I had purchased them from Farlows, and Graham actually went down there and went through all the old ticket stubs until he found the counterfoil for my rod licences. He was so convinced that I hadn't bought any and that I was trying to pull the wool over his eyes, even though I knew he had checked me down at Farlows. John Stent who was running Farlows at the time couldn't believe the trouble that this guy was going to, but it was all going to come to a head and get a lot worse for me as time went on.

After fishing on the Car Park Lake for a couple of seasons, a few of us decided to have a go on Colnemere. As this was a SSSI water with no fishing allowed, stealth was to be a major factor. I purchased a small camping bed, a waterproof cover for my sleeping bag, camouflaged the rods, reels, bank sticks etc, and dug myself in for a session in search of the Black Mirror. It was on only my second session up there, while walking back from the shop with Terry Hearn, that I met Graham face to face coming the opposite way back from the lake towards the car park. Graham took one look at me and ran as fast as he could, past Terry and me, on his way back to phone the police. I looked at Terry and Terry looked at me, and I said, "Uh-oh, we're in trouble now; that's Graham and he's got a vendetta against me. He's not going to let this go."

Sure enough, half an hour later the police turned up. I tried to explain to them that we were passionate about catching big carp; there was a big carp in the lake, and we were fishing for it. The policeman seemed to understand my passion, but some weeks later the summons arrived and I was done for fishing in the closed season, fishing a SSSI water, fishing three rods and unattended rods. So all in all, bingo – a full house.

To be honest, that was the catalyst that broke my fishing commitment. I was so fed up with the reaction from Graham that I decided to have a rest

Mid-thirty common off the top.

And another!

Two-tone upper thirty.

38lb-plus February common.

Swan brace.

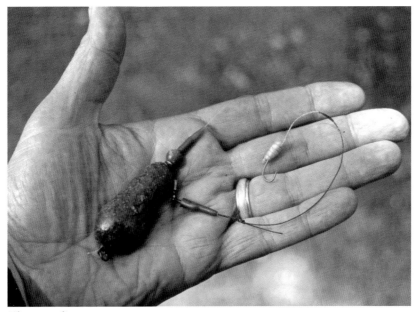

The mag-aligner.

Forty-plus common brace.

Nokia brace.

Swan chunk.

Charlie's Mate.

Horeshoe haulin'.

Zip brace.

Maylin's common, Pit 4 Frimley.

Charlie brace!

Immaculate.

Scaly Frimley mirror.

Pecs.

And another.

Pad Lake mid-thirty.

Sandhurst's Friendly Mirror.

Bubble Tail.

Countdown.

Scaly.

Nigel's.

Rosie.

Sergeant.

Kurt.

334 BIG CARP LEGENDS – ROB MAYLIN

from fishing, and in fact hung the rods up for the next three years. But as they say, once you can ride a bike, you never forget, and sure enough a few years later the capture of a near 40lb common from a lake not ten minutes from where I live spurred me into going and looking out a floater rod and purchasing a bag of Pedigree Chum mixers. Swan Valley had opened its doors to me; a lake I had never fished before, but one that now contained a 40lb common, something I dearly wanted to catch.

The fishing on Swan Valley was fast and furious, especially in the summer while fishing on the top with the floating dog biscuits. I had three 30lb commons in a day in my first week of fishing. Rob McGill, my great fishing pal, was soon to join me, and we had some of the most enjoyable fishing of our lives down there. Come the winter though it was a different story, and the fishing became very, very difficult using conventional methods.

I had been using maggots, and only just recently made a film for Rob Hughes down at Mayfields Lake using maggots and grubs. I landed about 15 carp that day and made my mind up to persevere with them on Swan. A couple of other friends of mine were also using maggots; Mick Elborough up in Cambridge had been using plastic maggots, and we'd been chatting on the phone about it, but it was Bernie Lofters who came up with the original idea for me to formulate the mag-aligner. Bernie caught three carp one day using a PVA bag of maggots combined with one of the Enterprise plastic maggots on a nylon hooklink. It was from his idea that I designed the mag-aligner rig, simply turning the plastic maggot round the other way and changing the hooklink material so that it was flexible within an inch or so of the hook. I combined that with the heli-line system for holding a stocking bag of maggots on the bottom of the lead, thus making it aerodynamic and accurately castable up to distances of 70-80 yards with conventional tackle.

Bernie always thinks I stole his idea, but I've always said that all ideas come in stages. It wasn't the man who invented the wheel who invented the bicycle, but in fact the man who invented the other wheel, and that's how I look at Bernie's invention of the maggot rig and my adaptation, the mag-aligner. Yes of course I owe it to Bernie, and I'm first to admit that, but I also owe it to Mick Elborough for giving me the idea of using plastic maggots in the first place, so to those two, thanks. You caught me lots of fish, guys.

Once I had developed the mag-aligner and created what I feel is one of the most effective hooking arrangements ever invented (not quite on par with the hair rig, but certainly not far behind), I went from strength to strength on a variety of waters. Swan Valley was the first, and the catches were incredible. At this time I was only doing day sessions, but I went from catching one carp every two or three day sessions down at Swan to catching eight or ten carp every time I went down there, such was this incredible change in my fishing and the number of fish caught. I ended up with over thirty thirties from the venue that season, and I caught the 40lb common twice.

Frimley was next on the hit list, but for those of you who have read Big Carp over the years, or even One Last Cast, my last book for that matter, you'll know that my time on Frimley was very short; so short in fact that I'm thinking of having another dabble back down there. There are some fantastic upper thirty fully scaled mirrors in there that I didn't catch. However, in the week that I fished down there, I did catch the three biggest commons in the lake – Charlie's Mate at 42lb, Charlie at 37lb and Pecs at 37lb along with about 40 other fish. It was an incredible week of day sessions, which people who fish the venue are talking about even now.

An invitation from Tim Wagner to have a go down at Horseshoe Lake with the maggots led me down there for three or four day sessions, and I had some fantastic results down there as well. It's one of the most beautiful complexes in the world, and I only wish it was a bit closer to home, as I'd certainly love to spend some more quality time down on that venue.

So we're almost up to date on my fishing. Sandhurst of course was the last of the venues for the mag-aligner, and I spent a couple of seasons down there fishing for its scaly residents. I missed out on one of the big ones, Cracker, which unfortunately died the first year I was down there. I was fortunate enough to catch an incredible number of thirties though, including the very sought after Nigel's Fish, Scaly and Countdown, three of the big mirrors, along with Bubble Tail, the lake's big common. Once again, if people want to read about the captures and how I went about it, there's plenty written about it in One Last Cast.

As you can see I have included pictures of all the big Swan, Frimley and Sandhurst fish at the end of this chapter. I don't intend to go into detail about their captures, these can all be found in One Last Cast, but if I didn't include them, I felt that I had not done justice to these beautiful fish from three tremendous waters. For those of you fed up with seeing my face on the last 20 pages, I apologise for catching so many, but I really couldn't bring myself to leave them out of this book.

So before my final note, I've got to mention Stuart Gillham's incredible lake in Krabi, Thailand. Stuart and I go way back to Harefield when we spent some great times together fishing the Colne Valley and wining and dining in the Horse and Barge. In the early 90s, Stuart went out to Thailand, where he started by doing marlin fishing trips and owning a couple of boats. In later years, he purchased some land in Krabi, dug a lake and made an oasis, one of the most incredible lakes in the world, if not the most incredible. It boasts about 15 world record species, contains fish up to 400lb in weight, has five-star accommodation, a restaurant and pub, and I've had some fantastic times out there both on the lake and in the town as well, where anything goes.

As for the future, well, I've already said, Frimley's got to be back on the hit list at some point. I certainly miss the mystery of carp fishing in the early days when you would go on a lake and not know what was in there, how big they were and what their names were. I thought for a long while that that side of carp fishing had gone forever, but in recent times, I have heard of some incredible captures from private estate lakes and pheasant farms that are opening my eyes up to carp fishing again. Certainly the thought of getting off the beaten track and catching an uncaught monster is high on my priority list. Like everyone though, we're all looking for that dream water, and perhaps one day I will find it.

Until then, I raise my glass to you all out there. Cheers guys, and may your next one be the one!